Candles in the Dark

Candles in the Dark

A Treasury of the World's Most Inspiring Parables

Todd Outcalt

John Wiley & Sons, Inc.

To Bill and Marilyn

Contents

Preface

While I was putting the finishing touches on *Candles in the Dark,* I was also struggling with the aftermath of the terrorist attacks that took place the morning of September 11, 2001. Like most Americans, I felt an evaporation of spirit while watching the horrifying images on television. Given the stark reality of such a tragedy, suddenly this book seemed so small and insignificant.

However, as people around the world began to grieve and grapple with the meaning of these events—and as I listened to some people who expressed hatred of others based on religion, creed, nationality, or race—I realized that this book could be an offering of hope and reconciliation in the post–September 11 world. The work of peace is ever before us, and I want to do my part by offering some stories of profound insight and wisdom— stories which are Jewish and Christian, Islamic and Buddhist, African and Native American, told by rich and poor over centuries of time.

I truly believe these stories can help us to light our own candles in the darkness of ignorance, hatred, and apathy, and can encourage us to embrace the best that is within each of us.

Author's Note

Most of the parables in this book are paraphrases of classic stories compiled from a variety of sources—both written and oral. In many instances, my rendition of the parables was originally told before live audiences in a variety of settings, and I frequently changed the language and structure of a particular parable to make it more understandable or enjoyable to a modern audience.

As a pastor, I have also used many of these parables in my work to offer insights and encouragement. Through the years, I have learned the value of these stories in addressing many aspects of the human condition.

I was also able, at long last, to utilize my background in classical studies for my own translations of the tales of Avianus. I used the Loeb Classical Library text of the Minor Latin Poets, and attempted to render the poetry of Avianus in a readable prose form for this work.

While not all of these stories would be classified in the narrowest sense as parables, I have selected fables, folktales, and moralistic stories that provide a strong teaching moment or insight. As such, I hope these are the greatest parables assembled in a single collection to date.

My hope was to offer a definitive collection of the world's greatest parables—from different cultures, times, and religious traditions—that would provide the general reader a comprehensive and fascinating glimpse of these timeless stories. I hope to have completed the task with some clarity and insight.

Several of these parables were originally published in somewhat different forms at http://www.fatbrain.com.

Every effort was made to trace copyright holders of works—
where these existed. However, since many of these stories come
from traditional or ancient sources, this effort proved to be most
challenging. If any unintended omissions have occurred, I would
ask for your forgiveness and would like to hear from you. I would
be happy to make appropriate acknowledgments in future editions of the work.

Acknowledgments

This book could not have been written without the support of many fine people, who also provided encouragement along the way.

My thanks to Tom Miller, who saw promise in this idea and helped me to craft the concept into a much richer book, offering perceptive insights and editorial guidance. Additional thanks to Elizabeth Zack, who persevered with me through some trying months and a mountain of questions while I was doing research for the book. Her expertise during the final stages of the book was invaluable and she continued to hold up the hope that all would be well. I am also grateful to Mark Steven Long for his guidance en route to the final manuscript, and to Diana Drew for her meticulous eye for detail and for cleaning up my messy prose.

I also thank my agent, Madeleine Morel, who not only guided me through this idea and stayed with the proposal through some doubtful months, but also created the perfect title.

Thanks to Valerie Traore and the African student body at the University of Indianapolis for passing along some wonderful tales and parables from their homelands, and to the people of University Heights United Methodist Church in Indianapolis.

I would also like to acknowledge those publishers granting permission to use copyrighted material. In particular, a rare little volume of Buddhist literature from Japan—*The Teaching of Buddha* (Bukkyo Dendo Kyokai, 1966)—proved to be a most inspiring source of traditional Buddhist tales.

Most of all, I thank my family—Becky, Chelsey, and Logan—who not only made the sacrifices necessary for the completion of the book, but continue, every day, to fill my life with new stories. I love you.

Introduction

Among the voluminous sources of Buddhist literature, there are many references attributed to the Buddha that begin with the phrase, "Now let me tell you a parable . . . " These words might remind Christians of the varied stories of the New Testament gospels that begin with the phrase, "Then Jesus told them a parable" or, in the earlier Jewish scriptures and oral rabbinical traditions, "Once there was a man who . . . "

Parables, for all of their brevity and density, possess a universal appeal and often extend beyond the religious, social, and historic milieus in which they were first spoken or written. As such, we find in parables both enlightenment and entertainment, for stories have the ability to move the heart as well as the imagination.

This book is meant to be such a collection—a journey of the soul as well as the mind. The parables represented in this book are by no means exhaustive of any culture or faith, but they do represent some of the finest from the great traditions of the past, including Buddhist, Jewish, Christian, Hindu, Native American, and African. Also included are tales gathered from the traditions of Sufism (Islamic mysticism), Hassidism, and from Taoist texts, among others. Many Yiddish parables that have been handed down orally for centuries have only recently been put into writing, and many Christian teachers have attempted to use the parable as a teaching method over the centuries, including the sizable collection of parables attributed to the Desert Fathers.

As you read through this collection, you will note that I have attempted to order the parables by topic. However, parables, like all great stories, often defy definition and contain a surplus of meaning—which is to say that they can address many facets of life simultaneously. The lessons and insights one gains from reading a parable one day may be missing in the next reading, and a new set of insights found in their stead. In this way, many a parable has sustained and challenged even the brightest and most revered students of every religious tradition or clan. Parables are timeless, and this is why they have been told around the campfire for centuries, each generation deriving a new set of lessons from them.

Adherents of a particular faith may note that I have sometimes abbreviated or lengthened a particular parable. Others may be written in a style that differs from the original or they may be taken out of the context in which the parable actually appears in a sacred text or tradition. For the purposes of this collection, many times I have taken certain liberties with the writing, offering my own paraphrases of these parables. I did so with the intent of offering the fruits of their wisdom and insights to a wider audience, in a style that is easily understandable and appreciated. No disrespect is intended, and I have made every attempt to maintain the integrity of the central aim or purpose of these stories. Taken within the context of a particular faith, however, I know that a parable can mean one thing within a religious tradition, and quite another outside of it. Nonetheless, I hope that this collection can add to the dialogue between people of differing persuasions and may be a source of inspiration to those who seek wisdom and insights for living, regardless of the source. As such, this collection is for anyone who seeks to live well, or who simply enjoys a good story.

It should be noted that not all parables seek to fulfill a religious purpose. Some parables—particularly in the Buddhist and Jewish traditions—may simply illustrate some aspect of life, such as marriage, or the nature of friendship, or answer more mundane questions about everyday living. Many Native American and African stories (not always parabolic in nature) have little to do with the great moral questions of life, but rather address observations about the natural world or questions regarding the history of one's clan or tribe. But these stories contain many truths about the nature of beauty, or freedom, or the importance of living in community with others. I hope they add to our own need for community and acceptance.

The word *parable* (meaning, literally, "to set beside" or "to compare") is a Greek term, commonly found throughout the Christian New Testament gospels. But the origin of parabolic storytelling has its roots in the more ancient Jewish faith. Following the exile in Babylon (after 586 B.C.E.) and the destruction of the first temple in Jerusalem, the Jewish people were forced to establish houses of prayer (synagogues) to keep their religious traditions and customs alive. Religious teachers, or rabbis, continued to interpret the Torah (law) for the people. These rabbinical teachings and interpretations of Jewish law were later collected into one work, known as the Mishnah, around 200 C.E. Later rabbis discussed the interpretation of these oral laws in a body of work known as the Gemara. Together these two make up the Talmud. The Talmud contains a wealth of ancient teachings— among them parables and stories—which the rabbis used to illustrate finer points of the law or other aspects of life.

Taken as a whole, this vast collection of Jewish literature and oral tradition is unrivaled in the number of parables and moral stories among the world's faiths. Later Jewish teachers such as the Hassidim and Jewish philosophers such as Martin Buber (1878–1965) also used the parable as a teaching method. You will no doubt find that this sizable corpus of Jewish parables is reflected in the makeup of this book.

The Jewish parables in this collection reflect the oral traditions of the early rabbis and later interpretations and stories collected in the Talmud. Later generations also used story to illustrate finer points of the Torah, or to illuminate or comment upon social difficulties. The Hassidic movement in eighteenth-century Europe was one such tradition that became rich with parables. Still later, Jews living in Poland and Russia, in particular, blended Hebrew and German into a language known as Yiddish. As late as the 1920s in America, Yiddish newspapers, books, and tales were widely circulated in the Jewish community and many of these parables were passed from one generation to the next.

Taoism also relies heavily on the use of parable for teaching and instruction. As a philosophy, Taoism originated in China some three hundred years before the Common Era (C.E.). *Tao*, meaning "way" or "path," also embraces the nuances of doctrine, method, principle, and order. As such, *Tao* has come to represent the source of all things, the matrix of existence, or the

Way. The Tao took written form over two thousand years ago in two collections: *Tao Te Ching* and *Chuang-tzu*. These two works, now regarded as classics of world literature, contain the compilations of ancient wisdom and mysticism illustrating the Tao. *Chuang-tzu,* in particular, contains many parables and moral stories that have lent themselves to various interpretations and traditions, including Taoist, Buddhist, Confucian, and various forms of Legalist and Martial schools of thought, including Zen. A wide selection of these Taoist, Buddhist, and Confucian parables, in particular, are included in this collection.

As for Christian parables, it is noteworthy to point out that Jesus himself was a rabbinical Jew, and as such spoke from the tradition and culture of the first-century storytellers, a common method of teaching at the time. Many of the parables of Jesus, however, could be regarded as some of the most well-known stories in the Western world. In addition to these parables, Christianity has also produced other parabolic traditions, such as the Desert Fathers (see pages 54–55), and, more recently, the parabolic stories of Søren Kierkegaard (1813–1855), a Danish philosopher regarded as the father of Christian existentialism.

Although Islam is the youngest of the great monotheist faiths, Muslim thought has nevertheless produced several major traditions and a fine collection of parabolic stories, most commonly in connection with Sufism, the mystical tradition of the faith. While many of the stories are far too lengthy to include in a collection like this, they are fine examples of the didactic method of storytelling. I have made several attempts in this volume to include abbreviated Islamic parables that are representative of the great storytelling art of the Sufis.

One will also note that among the numerous Native American legends there are parabolic stories that help us to appreciate the mysterious link between human life and the natural order, between life and death, and between the peoples of the earth. These parables, like Aesop's fables of old, often use animals and the forces of nature as the central characters of the tale, but their depth and insight is tremendous. Likewise, much that falls within the realm of African folklore has the central elements of earthiness, of fire and wind and rain. Other African tales are delightful moralistic stories or family sagas that can be appreciated by people of all ages, and were probably told around the campfire to teach the young.

As you read this volume, I hope you will do so with an open heart and a willing mind. Parables have a way of sneaking up on us, appealing to our secret senses, and delighting us in their simplicity of truth. One does not have to be a scholar or an academic to appreciate a parable. In fact, a literal mind is often an impediment to understanding a parable. Rather, what is required is a childlike imagination and the ability to think metaphorically.

In addition, you may also note that some of the parables in this collection sound vaguely familiar, or may have counterparts in other traditions and cultures. This is no surprise. Among oral traditions especially, many stories were swapped back and forth by various travelers. Sometimes it is difficult to tell where, exactly, a story originated. There are Buddhist parables that have been retold in a Christian context, and African stories that were used by Jewish teachers, among others. Therefore, the original source of a given parable is often lost in the telling and the retelling.

What is important is the significance of the parable—the story itself. If we listen closely enough, we might discover something new about ourselves or our world.

❧

On a personal note, I would like the reader to know that I have been collecting parables for many years. Like many, I grew up cutting my teeth on Aesop's fables, and then graduated to more complex moralistic and religious tales as my understanding of the world broadened. A list of the primary sources I used for this book appears in the bibliography, and I would like to thank the authors and editors of these books for adding to my knowledge of the subject of parables and their meanings. My aim was to choose the best parables from a cross-section of cultures, traditions, and religions that would provide the reader with a definitive collection of these stories. I hope that my paraphrases of the stories will also add a new dimension to the art of storytelling.

Likewise, I hope my brief commentaries following each parable will prove helpful and insightful. In much the same way a parable was often used to cast light on a particular argument or question, I want to offer a few thoughts that might help the reader dig into the story or better understand the religious or cultural background of the tale. These commentaries are by no means exhaustive, but are personal reflections meant to offer the reader some additional insights.

❧

For the ancient rabbis, the value of a parable resided in its ability to teach. Often the parables themselves grew to have a significance and tradition of their own and came to be remembered outside the classical debate in which they originated.

In Jewish tradition, the moral story, or parable, was often used to illustrate the significance of the parable itself, as in this example:

> Don't consider a parable to be worthless. Through the use of a story, you can understand even the deepest truths. Think of a king who misplaced a gold coin or a pearl—he might be able to find it by using the light from a wick worth no more than a penny. Therefore, pay attention to a parable—by its light you may be able to understand the ways of life.

So read these parables. But more than that, use them as candles in the dark. Let them offer light and direction. In so doing you will be richly rewarded.

Or perhaps, as this classic Jewish tale suggests, the reward may simply be the story itself.

> The Baal Shem Tov, when he had a problem, used to go into the forest to pray at a specific place. Here he would light a fire and offer his petitions to God.
>
> After the Baal Shem Tov died, his successor followed this same pattern—going to the place in the forest to pray. However, he did not light a fire. "After all," he said, "we do not know how the master lit his fire. But we can still pray."
>
> A generation later, Rabbi Moshe Lieb went to the place in the forest. But he said, "We do not know how to light the fire, nor do we know how the prayer was said, but we know this holy place in the forest. That is enough."
>
> A generation after this, Rabbi Israel of Rishen no longer journeyed to the holy place to pray. He said, "The fire we cannot light. The prayer we no longer know. And the place where the master prayed is lost to us. All we can do now is tell the story."

Candles in the Dark

Some pupils came to the rabbi complaining about the prevalence of evil in the world. They asked the rabbi how they might drive out the darkness. The rabbi gave them brooms, and asked them to sweep the darkness from a cellar. The pupils tried this, but they were not successful. So the rabbi gave them sticks and told them to beat the darkness until it was driven away. Again they tried, and when they failed, the rabbi asked them to try shouting at the darkness. The pupils did this also, but the darkness remained. "Then let us try this," the rabbi said. "Let each person challenge the darkness by lighting a candle." The pupils descended into the cellar. Each one lit a candle. When they looked about, they discovered that the darkness had disappeared.

1

Family Matters

These are the duties of obligation . . . between father and son, between husband and wife, and those which are shared between brothers.

—Confucius

Through the years, I have often had the privilege of being one of the first people to welcome a new child into the world. Likewise, I am often invited to be with grieving families following the death of a loved one. I say this is a privilege because there are few occupations or callings in life that afford a person so much intimacy with families in moments of highest joy and deepest sorrow. To be invited into the home or hospital room, to sit at a table and share a meal, to speak words of celebration or comfort—all of these moments can be profound and meaningful.

During funeral services, I like to remind people that we were not only created as individuals, but as families. When you and I think about our center of warmth (that place in the heart from which we draw strength and nurturing and love), we most often see faces of family members and we think about remembered times and special moments with those whom we love. Every individual—in one way or another—cherishes family, longs for intimacy, and yearns for peace within the home.

Throughout the centuries, storytellers and teachers have recounted simple tales of family joys, family heartaches, and the ties that make a house a home. In every culture and tongue, there are parables that remind us of the universal need for family, the yearning we have for simple moments in the home, and the joys of being a parent, a child, a spouse, a sister, or a brother.

The parables in this chapter are profound reminders of the ties that bind us together. Some parables celebrate the joys of life; others contemplate the sorrows. Some parables carry us along and give us a smile; others challenge our perceptions and our comforts.

As you read the parables in this chapter, I hope you will find a few to live by, and a few that will help you to nourish the spirit of your home. May these simple stories help you to cherish *your* center of warmth.

The Road to Heaven
(Jewish)

Years ago there lived a man who had grown very tired of his life and his family. And so he decided he would set out on a journey to heaven where he would live in happiness, free of all worries and cares.

Early one morning he said goodbye to his wife and children. Leaving town, he walked for three straight days until he grew weary and decided to stop for a nap. Sitting down beside the road, the fellow took off his shoes and pointed them in the direction he had been walking so that, when he awoke, he would embark on his journey in the right direction.

Now, as it happened, a trickster came walking down the road as the man was asleep. Seeing the man's shoes along the side of the road, the trickster stopped, picked them up, and set them down again, pointing them in the opposite direction. When the fellow awoke, he put on his shoes and set off on his journey again, not realizing that he was backtracking every step of the way.

After a couple of days, the man noticed that much of the terrain began to look vaguely familiar. "Surely I must be approaching heaven," he said, "for I have been told that heaven has a familiar beauty to it."

A day later, the man approached a town. "What a nice place," the man said to himself. When he passed along the streets, he noticed that many of the people looked like friends and smiled at him. He found a house that looked much like the one he had built. He knocked on the door. A woman and children—looking much like the family he had left behind—appeared at the door and welcomed him.

This man went into the house and dwelt there in happiness all the days of his life.

• • •

Every individual, at one time or another, feels a restlessness in life—a desire for something greater, for something more. A person can grow weary of routine, of seeing the same faces around the dinner table, of having the same conversations. In essence, we want more out of life, so we search for a greater happiness.

However, as this parable reveals, happiness is never far away, but, rather, can be found in the everyday spaces of life and among the people we need and love the most. True joy is not a prize to be discovered, but the happiness that can be created each day.

As in life, there are many paths that one may take to discover the secret of joy. Many of these, however, circle back to the source of that joy—family, home, familiar faces, and familiar times.

The journey, of course, is what makes this discovery so amazing. Often, in the far country, we realize what has been lost. The return is only a first step away. And the lessons we learn on the journey home are the blessings that can last a lifetime.

Enough Fish
(Yiddish)

Long ago a poor man and woman had nine children. This made eleven people—all of them living together in a small house.

Life was difficult, and the father used to go to the river every evening after a long day's work to fish for the family dinner. But, try as he might, he never caught more than eleven fish at one time. This meant that everyone in the family was able to eat just one fish for supper.

Every day the man would pray, "O Lord, how is it possible for a person to satisfy his hunger with only one fish?"

As time went by, the man began to have other thoughts about the fish, and he wondered how he might obtain a second fish for his own dinner. There were days when he even pondered the possibility of having a death in the family so that he might enjoy two fish instead of one. He was not an evil man, but was merely trying to assuage his own hunger.

Day after day he went to the river, but always he returned with eleven fish. Then one day the man received word that one of his children had died.

Naturally, he was deeply saddened by this loss. But, soon afterwards, the thought came into his head that he would, at last, have an extra fish to eat.

The next day, when the man went to the river, he was sad, but cheered by the one thought of what awaited him for supper that night. However, that day he caught only ten fish.

The man said to himself, "When I caught eleven fish, I was happy, and God provided. Now I catch only ten. So what have I accomplished?"

•   •   •

The lessons of this parable go far beyond greed and self-satisfaction. The greater need is to appreciate the gifts we have been given.

In life, it is often the case that we take for granted those blessings that are closest to us, that we see every day. These gifts tend to become invisible. And yet, when they are taken away, we feel sadness and loss.

This parable holds promise for those who have experienced loss in life, or who have a special need for tangible signs of love. In the end, this parable promises that there will always be enough—no matter what the loss—and there will always be a supply equal to meet any need.

The Reunion
(Buddhist)

Once upon a time there was a wealthy man who had an only son. The son left home, but soon became impoverished. When word of the son's condition reached the father, the father left home and began to search far and wide for his child. He wandered over the face of the earth, far from home, but could never locate his son. Finally, reduced to sorrow, the father returned home.

Now it came to pass that, years later, the son being wretched and reduced to nothing, wandered near his father's home by chance, but he had no memory of his upbringing. When the father recognized his son, he sent his servants to bring the boy home. However, when the son saw the mansion and the beautiful grounds, he was overcome with awe and would not return with the servants, for he feared that they were deceiving him.

So the father sent back servants and told them to offer his son money if he would come to work in the mansion. Hearing their offer, the son accepted, and became a servant in his father's house.

Through the course of weeks, the father gradually promoted his son until he was put in charge of all of the father's worldly goods. Yet the son still did not recognize his own father. However, the father was so pleased with his son's faithfulness that, as the father's life drew to a close, he gathered together all of his servants, friends, and relatives and said, "This is my only son, the son I searched for all those years. From this day, all of my possessions and worldly goods belong to him."

Now, when the son heard this, he came to his senses and said, "At last I have found my father, for all that he has is now mine."

•   •   •

Love is the bond that binds a family together, and love alone allows us to triumph over the sorrows and inequalities of life, even when we do not understand the nature of another's sacrifices. These are the lessons of this parable.

On another level, this story is much like Jesus's parable of the prodigal son who left home, only to be accepted again by the loving parent. Beyond the relationship itself is a greater love.

Many people who have been harmed or injured by love discover that memories can be painful. When someone we love has hurt us, there is a tendency to forget the past, including many of the good things we enjoyed.

But remembering also brings peace and reconciliation—if not with others, at least within ourselves. The ability to forgive another person is the first step in finding personal wholeness. True intimacy and love cannot be obtained until one learns to forgive the past and embrace the future with confidence.

A Common Good
(Jewish/Yiddish)

This is a story about a man who lost everything and became so poor that he was forced to earn his living by plowing other people's fields. One day, while he was busy plowing, the prophet Elijah appeared to him and said, "You will be blessed with seven good years. Would you like to have them now, while you are still young? Or later, when you are old?"

The poor man dismissed the prophecy, since he believed the prophet Elijah to be a sorcerer. But three days later the prophet appeared to him again and asked the same question.

The poor man was astonished and said, "I beg you, please let me go home and ask my wife." So he ran home and told his wife that the prophet Elijah had appeared to him and had told him that he was to enjoy seven years of plenty.

"Let's take the seven good years now," she said. "After all, we don't know what might become of us when we are old."

And so the man went back to the field and again the prophet appeared to him. "I will take the seven good years now," he told the prophet.

"So be it," said Elijah. "Return to your home, and when you get there, you will be blessed with great wealth."

Now it happened that the poor man's children were playing in a pile of dung that very afternoon and they accidentally discovered a treasure—enough money to feed their entire family for seven years. When they realized what had happened, they began to praise God. And the wife said, "Truly God has been gracious to us and sent us seven good years. But let us not forget to practice piety and generosity during these seven years of plenty, for it may be that God, blessed be his name, will be compassionate to us later."

And so they practiced generosity and kindness, sharing their wealth with many people.

When the seven good years were almost finished, again the prophet Elijah appeared to the man and said, "The time has come for me to take back what God has given you. I want you to return the money."

But the man said, "Again, I pray you, let me consult with my wife on this matter." And with that word the fellow returned to his house and told his wife that the prophet had come to take back the money of the seven good years.

His wife told him, "Go tell the prophet that he may have the money if he is able to find a family more charitable than we have been. If he is able, then we will restore the money."

Now God noted the woman's words and took note of the wonderful works that she and her husband had performed. And God rewarded them with even more wealth.

•   •   •

A generous person understands that one gains more wealth from giving to others than from hoarding riches. Generosity, in all its forms, always gives back.

Few people pause to consider, however, the generosity that a family can offer together. A family working together for a common good is a blessing to the community around them.

The parable also demonstrates that God is fair. Those who seek to be a blessing to others have every right to request God's assistance. As long as one sees the blessings of riches and wealth as an honor, not an entitlement, true joy will be found in the acts of charity, the service one renders to a needy world.

The Ways of Home
(A parable of the Buddha)

Hear the parable of a good home. A family is a place where minds come into contact with each other. If these minds love one another, the home will be as beautiful as a flower garden. But if these minds get out of harmony with one another, it is like a storm that wreaks havoc upon the beauty of that sacred place.

•   •   •

Harmony in the home is not cultivated by chance or luck. Building a family takes work, time, effort—as with the tending of a garden. Likewise, trouble can come from many corners. When one fails to be attentive to a husband, wife, or child, the seeds of disharmony begin to be sown.

As this parable demonstrates, the secret to a harmonious family is to give focused attention to the important matters of the heart. Respect, courtesy, dignity—these virtues are the ones healthy families pass along from one generation to the next. They are the cornerstones of love. A home must be nurtured if one expects to see maturity and growth—the transformation of love into a thing of beauty.

Reconciliation
(Buddhist)

Once there lived a man of deep faith who, after his father died, lived happily with his mother before taking a wife. At first the man and his wife lived happily together under the same roof with the mother, but then, after a silly misunderstanding, the wife and her mother-in-law became estranged and grew to resent each other. The situation became so bad that finally the mother left the house, leaving the young couple to fend for themselves.

Soon the woman had a child. She told a neighbor, "You see, when my mother-in-law lived with us, nothing good ever happened. But as soon as she left the house, we were blessed with a child."

Now it happened that this word got back to the mother-in-law. She grew bitter and said, "If the husband's mother is forced from the home before a blessing takes place, this is quite an injustice. What is the world coming to?"

The mother-in-law was so filled with hatred toward her son's wife that she decided to go to the cemetery and hold a funeral service, counting her daughter-in-law as dead. But when a god heard of this, he appeared to the woman and tried to reason with her. However, the woman was not to be dissuaded. "So be it then," the god said. "But I warn you: I must burn the child and the mother to death."

When she heard her own hatred echoed in the voice of the god, the woman realized her mistake, apologized for her anger, and begged the god to spare the life of the wife and child. At this same time, the son and his wife realized their mistake in turning the mother away and went to the cemetery to seek her out. This family came to life again and was reconciled in the place of the dead.

• • •

What family has not experienced estrangement and heartache at some time? Misunderstandings arise, harsh words are spoken, feelings are bruised. But the little things of life have a way of being blown out of proportion. Small disagreements and words spoken in anger often come back to harm us in the end.

However, as this parable reminds us, forgiveness is essential—especially with regard to family relationships. Little hurts and petty arguments melt away when we are faced with a crisis in the family. In essence, no family can survive without forgiveness and there is always room in our hearts for reconciliation, especially when we realize the truth of the old adage: Blood is thicker than water.

As in many parables, the cemetery is a reminder not only of our final destination, but of what is important in life. It is a far greater act to love someone in life, than to love someone in death.

On Children
(Confucian)

Confucius said, "Consider a healthy family. When you do something for your parents, try to bring them along slowly. If you see they are unwilling to go along with your plans, respect their decision and do not try to force your will upon them; neither resent them for the time and trouble they may have caused you."

•   •   •

This little story—more wisdom, perhaps, than parable—is typical of the Confucian style of teaching, and is included here to demonstrate the diverse styles of wisdom to be found in various traditions. The famous Chinese teacher, born in 550 B.C.E., taught frequently on the matters of government and the state. But he was equally interested in teaching truths of the family—particularly with regard to husband/wife, father/son, older brother/younger brother, and friend/friend relationships.

As with many teachers of various cultural and religious persuasions, Confucius himself regarded one rule as governing all others in the home: "What you do not want done to yourself, do not do to others."

Likewise, Confucius believed in five basic virtues of the home: love, justice, reverence, wisdom, and sincerity. On these, he believed, hinged the basic form and function of the family.

One Heart, One Mind
(Buddhist)

An elderly couple once came to Buddha and asked, "Master, we were married early in life and have known each other since childhood. However, there has always been a cloud of unhappiness in our relationship. Please tell us if we can be remarried in the next life."

The Buddha replied, "If you have the same faith, receive the teaching in the same fashion, and if you have the same wisdom, then you will be of the same mind in the next birth."

• • •

Here, as with the Jewish and Christian concept of marriage, the goal of matrimony is for a couple to become as one. This singularity of purpose and heart comes with maturity and can be found, according to this parable, through a shared faith, an agreeable understanding of spiritual things, and a similar philosophy of life. This results in oneness.

Unhappiness, on the other hand, can often be traced to differences rather than similarities. The idea that opposites attract may be true in many cases, but successful marriages are always built on common goals and aspirations.

Great Aspirations
(Confucian)

Confucius said, "Herein lies a truth. Watch what a man aspires to while his father is still living. Then observe how he lives after his father has passed away. If he does not change his aspirations and manner of living for three years after his father's death, there is no doubt he loved his father."

• • •

Imitation, as they say, is the sincerest form of flattery. For a child to aspire to be like a parent may be natural, but it is not always expedient.

Imitation points to the higher virtues, according to Confucius. When a young child imitates a parent, this may be mimicry. But when adult children remain true to their upbringing and values after the death of a parent, this is a testament to the parent's goodness and love.

The goal of the parent is to live a virtuous life. In such a way, a child is given a foundation for the future. The greatest gift a parent can offer a child is an exemplary life.

The Backyard Marriage
(Jewish)

Once, a beautiful mouse was born. As he grew older, everyone in his family admired his good looks and his parents often asked themselves, "Where will we ever find a wife who is worthy of such a son?"

When the time came for the mouse to be wed, the parents decided that only God would know of a suitable lady mouse worthy of their son's good looks and charm. So, according to the custom, the oldest members of the mouse family went to see God. They knocked on God's door and waited.

After God had invited them in, they stated their business. "We represent the family of the beautiful mouse," they said, "a creature of such astounding beauty that you most surely have heard of him. We have decided that only you would know where we could find a wife worthy of his charms."

"Ah," God said. "It is true that this fellow must have the proper wife, but I am afraid you have come to the wrong place. You should consult with the family of the Wind, for the Wind is mightier than I."

"How can the Wind be mightier than God?" they asked.

God answered, "When the Wind blows, he covers the earth—which I have created—with dust."

After this, the family members consulted and decided that surely someone from the family of the Wind was worthy to marry the mouse. "Where is the house of the Wind?" they asked.

God directed them, and as soon as they arrived and knocked on the door of the Wind's house, the Wind welcomed them inside. "We have come to seek a wife for the finest mouse in the world," the family members told the Wind. "So we have come to ask for a daughter from your family."

The Wind listened, but answered, "What a wonderful idea! But I am afraid there is one more powerful than I. That is the Mountain. For you see, no matter how hard I blow, I cannot move the Mountain."

"Where can we find the house of the Mountain?" they asked.

The Wind directed the way, and as soon as they knocked on the door of the house of the Mountain, the Mountain welcomed them inside. They again explained why they had come.

"A wonderful idea!" the Mountain exclaimed. "But I am afraid there is one more powerful than I. He digs at my foundation day and night and makes holes in me. There is nothing I can do to keep him from wearing me down."

"A most powerful creature," the messengers said. "Where can we find him?"

The Mountain directed the family to a tiny house in the valley. The house was the home of a mouse. When the messengers knocked on the door and were welcomed inside, they explained why they had come. When the mouse family heard the offer they said, "This is wonderful. What a joy it is that our two families should be united by the marriage of our children."

•　　•　　•

This humorous tale, of course, has nothing to do with mice, but everything to do with human attitudes and prejudices—particularly with regard to family class and the vanities that can accompany marriage. What parents don't believe that their son or daughter is the greatest catch in the world?

In cultures where marriages are arranged, this story demonstrates through humor that one should never regard a son or daughter so highly that a match will be impossible to find. What parent wouldn't, after all, like to find a match arranged directly by God, a match made in heaven? But since such matches are rare, it is best to look for other alternatives.

At its heart, this delightful story is a reminder that true happiness and harmony can be found in our own backyards, and we don't have to go far to find true love!

Marital Riches
(Jewish)

Once a man came to his rabbi and said, "I have been married for ten years, but my wife and I have been unable to have children. I would ask that you grant me a certificate of divorce so that I might marry another and have a child to carry on my name."

Now the rabbi was wise and, seeing that the man was acting rashly, he asked him to go home and prepare a great feast for the divorce proceedings. "One should celebrate a divorce as one celebrates a marriage," the rabbi said.

Because the fellow was eager to please his rabbi, he went home and did as he was asked, preparing a fantastic party for the occasion. But as he ate and drank, he began to feel giddy and generous. He told his wife, "In honor of our impending divorce, I am prepared to give you the most valuable item in the house. You may have anything you desire. I wish you the best."

Later that night, after the guests had gone home and the party had died down, the man fell into a deep sleep. His wife had the servants carry him to her father's house. When the man awoke the next morning, he was shocked to find that he was sleeping in a strange bed. He demanded an explanation.

"I am doing as you requested," his wife said. "You offered me the most valuable thing in the house, and I have chosen you."

The man was deeply touched by his wife's love. The next day he went to the rabbi and said, "Rabbi, forgive me. Pray for us. Pray that God may grant us children."

The rabbi assured the man that he had been praying all along. Nine months later his wife gave birth to their first child.

• • •

One truth about life: life is not fair! Life rarely gives us all that we desire or hope for. There are failures and shortcomings. Likewise, no marriage is perfect, and there are many obstacles to overcome. However, it is good to know that above all of the misfortunes and struggles of life, we are loved. When we lose sight of this truth, we lose sight of all that is good and valuable.

In marriage, as in life, it is easy to focus attention on what we do not have, rather than what we already enjoy. Some blessings remain hidden until other people reveal them to us.

Likewise, we often get what we ask for, especially when we desire the best things.

The Lost and the Found
(African)

Once there was a brother and sister whose parents had died. They lived together in a small hut.

One day when the brother came home from the field, his sister said to him, "Two men were here yesterday. If you go away again, they are sure to kidnap me."

"Nonsense," the brother said. But the sister told him, "No! Listen to me! When they come for me, I will take a gourd full of sap and let it drip along the path so you will be able to find me." The brother, of course, dismissed his sister's fears, but the next day, when he came back from the field, she was gone!

Remembering his sister's plan, the young man began to follow the drops of sap. However, as the days wore on, the sap soon began to sprout into small trees and finally after days of searching, he was forced to return to his hut. Day after day he longed to find his sister, but his despair did nothing but increase his appetite. Each day he ate a goat from the flock until they were all gone. Then he ate the oxen, one by one. At last, years later, when there was nothing left to eat, he took heart again and set out again to find his sister.

Now by this time the tiny saplings had grown into giant trees. The brother followed them for days until he came to a small village where some children were playing. The man asked the children for a drink from their gourd. The oldest child said, "Give him a drink. For our mother has told us that if anyone asks for a drink from the gourd, he is her brother."

Later that day, after the children returned to their home, the man waited until their mother appeared. He was surprised to see that it was his long-lost sister. However, many years had passed, and his sister did not recognize him.

The next day, the man was with the children when he threw a stone toward a flock of birds and said, "Fly away birds, fly away! Just as my sister flew away from me many years ago."

The children were intrigued by these words and rushed back to their hut to tell their mother what the stranger had said. Their mother responded, "He is my brother! Bring him to me."

But when the children returned to the man with this message, he refused to come to their home, saying, "I have dwelt in the hut of my sister, but she has given me nothing to eat."

So she told her children, "Give him ten goats, then he will come."

But still he refused to come.

"Give him ten oxen," she said.

But still he refused to come.

"Send him ten cows," she said.

Still, he refused to be reconciled to his sister.

Finally, she said, "Give him forty more goats, forty more oxen, and forty more cows." And at last he relented and came to meet his sister. After they embraced she said, "I am sorry I did not recognize you before."

And so it was that after this the brother and sister were reconciled, the brother married a woman of the village and lived near the hut of his sister for the rest of his life.

•　　•　　•

Choices made at an early stage of life tend to shape the rest of our lives. Like the brother in the parable, we often lose our way. Life becomes a confusing twist and tangle of the unfamiliar. Trying to mend our ways can often be a difficult and time-consuming process, for life marches on. We have to take one step at a time, one day at time, if we are to see our way clear to our life's true destination.

This parable, however, includes the hope of reconciliation and forgiveness in family relationships. And, in families, these virtues are important for our well-being. As the story concludes, there is a sense in which one cannot be truly happy until one has made amends with the past.

The Greatest of All Illusions
(Buddhist)

Once there lived a great Tibetan teacher by the name of Marpa. Monks came from far and wide to study with him. One day Marpa received word that his eldest son had been killed, and he began to grieve deeply. When the monks saw the sorrow of their master they said, "We do not understand. You have taught us that all is an illusion. Yet you are grieving for the loss of your son. How do you explain this?"

Marpa answered them, "Yes, everything is an illusion. And the death of a child is the greatest illusion of all."

• • •

The loss of a loved one transcends religious belief. The sense of loss we feel, more than any doctrine or creed, is a testament to the universal power of love and the primacy of family relationships. There is also the recognition in all cultures that life is transient and fleeting. To make the most of life, we must exercise our hearts as well as our beliefs. Learning to live each moment to the fullest with those we love is the very essence of life itself. When a loved one is taken away, no religious faith can completely assuage or mend the loss.

The Internal Compass
(Buddhist)

A grandfather and his granddaughter—who made their living performing as acrobats—came to the Buddha for advice. "How can we best care for each other while we are performing dangerous stunts?" they asked.

The grandfather contended that it was best for each of them to be aware of the safety of the other, and, in this way, they would most likely remain free from harm. The granddaughter, on the other hand, thought her grandfather had it backwards. "I believe that, if each of us is attentive to our own balance, we will best keep each other from harm," she said.

When the Buddha heard this, he said to the grandfather, "Though your granddaughter is young, she is wise. If you guard your own safety as a grandfather, you will also be guarding the safety of your granddaughter."

And to the granddaughter the Buddha added, "And if you, being a child, guard yourself with awareness, integrity, and respect, you will preserve both yourself and those around you."

•   •   •

Being faithful to one's self and one's ideas is crucial to success. And more than self-preservation is at stake: those who depend on us are also strengthened by our successes.

The secret to success, as the parable points out, is having an internal compass of integrity, self-awareness, and respect. When we are aware of our actions, there is a greater chance of harmony with others. When we have integrity, others trust us. And when others respect us, our confidence increases.

Those who treat themselves well will also be able to support others when it counts. The wise seek to strengthen themselves first, and, by doing so, are able to support others as a result.

The parable echoes the old adage: Better to do battle with a handful of the strong than with an army of the weak.

The Wise and the Old
(Buddhist)

Long ago, there was a country that had a custom of abandon-
ing its aged people in a remote wasteland. But a certain official
of the state rebelled against the custom when it was time for
him to abandon his father. Instead, the official built a secret,
underground cave. Here he hid his father, fed him, and provided for all his needs.

Now it came to pass that an emissary of God appeared
before the king of that country, offering a riddle and a stern
warning. "If you cannot solve the riddle," the emissary said,
"your country will be destroyed."

"What is the riddle?" the king asked.

"There are two snakes," came the riddle. "Tell me the sex
of each."

The king and his palace servants pondered the riddle for
days, but were unable to solve the problem. At last the king
offered a great reward to anyone in the kingdom who could
come up with the answer to the riddle.

Now when the official heard of the king's predicament,
he went to his father in the cave and asked, "There are two
snakes. How can you know the sex of each?"

The man's father said, "That is simple. Place the two
snakes on a soft carpet. The one that moves is the male. The
one that stays still is the female."

The official returned to the king, offered the answer, and
the riddle was solved. However, the next day, the godly emissary again appeared before the king with a more difficult
riddle: "Who is the one who, being asleep, is called the awakened one, and being awake, is called the sleeping one?"

Again the king and his servants were unable to answer.
And again the official asked his father in the cave, and
returned with the correct answer: "One who is under training
for Enlightenment."

In the days that followed, the emissary appeared before the king with far more difficult riddles such as:

"How can you weigh an elephant?"

"What does this mean: 'A cupful of water is more than the water of an ocean?' "

"There are two identical horses—how can you tell the mother from the daughter?"

And each time the official went to his father and received the answer. The first answer was, "Load the elephant on a boat and mark how deep the boat sinks into the water. Then remove the elephant and load the boat with stones until it sinks to the same level. Then unload the stones and weigh them."

The second answer was, "A cupful of water is given in compassion to a sick child or an aging parent, and thus, by its eternal spirit, has greater weight than all the water in the ocean."

And the third answer was, "Feed the horses hay. The horse that pushes the hay toward the other is the mother. The horse that receives it is the daughter."

Eventually the king was so impressed with the official's wisdom, he asked for the secret of his knowledge. The official admitted that he had hidden his father and all of the wisdom had come from him.

After hearing this, the king revoked the law of the wasteland and ordered that all elders be treated with kindness and respect.

•   •   •

On the surface, this is a parable dealing with the respect any society owes to its elders. But beyond the simple morality lesson, there are several keen insights that are worthy of note.

First, the elders of the land are those who possess wisdom and knowledge of the past, and have observed the fullness of life. The older members of a society have taken the time to observe the intricacies of nature—the way animals interact, the way compassion and kindness are extended. Their wisdom in these matters cannot be denied.

Second, the elders of the land are those who can often be ignored. The symbolism of the cave and the wasteland have particular meaning for a society that relegates the aged to places where they are largely unseen and unheard.

Finally, the parable demonstrates the importance of passing on wisdom and knowledge from one generation to the next. In this manner, the world is saved from destruction, from making the same mistakes time and again. A benevolent society is one in which all are respected, admired, and given an opportunity to contribute to the good of the whole.

❧

The Blessing of Grandchildren
(Jewish)

There was a wealthy man who had complete confidence in his son. During his lifetime, he transferred the entirety of his estate to his son's care.

When the son received this sudden wealth, however, he began to neglect his father—to the point where the father was left destitute, clothed only in rags. Meanwhile, the son himself had a family, and he had a son who was very kind and understanding.

One day the grandson was walking around town when he came upon his grandfather begging in the streets. He was surprised to see his grandfather in this condition, and asked if he could help him in any way. The grandfather replied, "Go to your father and ask him if I may have a blanket to keep myself warm."

The grandson went home immediately, retreated to the attic, and found a warm blanket. When his father asked him what he was doing, he said, "I am cutting a blanket in half."

"Why would you do that?" the father asked.

"I am giving half to my grandfather, so that he will have something to keep him warm. And the other half I am saving for you, so that when you are old, you will have a blanket as well."

When the father heard his son's reply, he realized how he had neglected his own father, went to him, and brought him into his home.

●   ●   ●

This parable may have originally been told to illustrate the commandment: "Honor your father and mother." But the story goes beyond the bond of fathers and sons, or mothers and daughters, to show how grandchildren can also be a blessing and an example. Caring for aging parents and relatives is one of the greatest challenges people face, and it is not always easy to know what to do.

Fortunately, we have a few excellent tales such as this one that demonstrate the nature of care, helpfulness, and the place of intergenerational love.

2

Faith to Live By

Cleave ever to the sunnier side of doubt,
And cling to Faith beyond the forms of Faith.

—Alfred Lord Tennyson

Regardless of one's observance, or nonobservance, of a particular faith, one could make a convincing argument that human beings are believers by nature. People desperately want to believe in something, or somebody, and the ways in which we perceive a great many aspects of life are often swayed by the convictions we hold with regard to things unseen. In essence, this is faith.

Faith, however, in the long strand of human history has, and continues to be, a source of both tension and cooperation among people. Faith can bring people together and, sadly, it can also drive people apart. Faith addresses both that which is to come, and that which is. And faith, in its highest nature, brings people into conflict with their own tendencies and failures, revealing their shortcomings and giving them a source of introspection, improvement, and forgiveness.

But there are other truths as well. Faith holds the possibility of opening up new worlds and fresh perspectives. Through delight and awe, wonderment and questioning, we often arrive at deeper places of the heart and learn to touch the things of God. Sometimes this comes only as we open ourselves to new realities, as we leave behind the old, and as we listen to the insights and

31

opinions of others. We can learn to be wise by becoming fool-ish. We can learn to move by standing still and listening. We can become free by taking upon ourselves the disciplines of service and self-sacrifice.

It would not be wrong to say that every religion or faith provides some or all of these insights in one form or another. The perspectives may be different, but there are some truths that transcend the particular tenets of a given faith.

As such, I hope that people of all faiths, or no faith, will find the parables of this chapter not only uplifting and inspiring, but also compelling in the simple truths and insights they con-vey. There is enough truth in this chapter for everyone, and I hope that these delightful stories will challenge even the most unwavering of convictions and the shallowest of hearts.

The Value of Life
(Jewish)

Many years ago a fugitive entered a small village and attempted to hide there from the authorities. The people, not knowing that he was a wanted man, were kind and generous. They provided for him and opened their hearts in hospitality. In fact, in time, they accepted him as one of their own. They grew to love him.

One afternoon a group of soldiers entered the village in search of the fugitive. They were certain the young man was hiding somewhere among the people. When no one offered to help the soldiers, or provide them with information about the fugitive, the soldiers grew angry. They threatened to kill the people and burn the village unless the young man was handed over to them.

The people were torn; they did not know what to do. They went to the village rabbi and asked for his advice. The rabbi was troubled. On the one hand he did not want to deliver the young man over to the authorities and a certain death. But on the other hand he did not want to see the people destroyed.

And so he decided to seek guidance through prayer and by searching the scriptures. All night long he read the Bible and prayed. Finally, as dawn was breaking, he happened upon these words in the Bible: "It is better that one man dies than that the whole people be lost."

Upon reading this, the rabbi closed his Bible and called the soldiers. He told them where the young man was hiding.

After the soldiers found the young man, they led him away to be killed, and the entire village joined together in a celebration, praising the rabbi because he had saved the people from destruction. However, the rabbi, overcome with a deep sadness because a human life had been taken, retired to his room and did not join the others in the celebration.

That night an angel of God visited the rabbi. The angel appeared to him and asked, "What have you done?"

The rabbi answered, "I handed over the fugitive to the enemy."

"But you have handed over the Messiah."

"How could I have known?" the rabbi cried.

The angel answered, "If, instead of reading the scriptures and praying, you had taken the time to visit the young man and look but once into his eyes, you would have known."

•   •   •

The expectation of a messiah, or anointed deliverer, can be found in many Jewish parables. In traditional Jewish lore, it is believed that the messiah would arrive on the day that every Jew observed the totality of the law. This parable, however, like many of its kind, is a reminder that God's purposes and plans are not always found in pious observances or strict interpretation of the scriptures. Personal experience and being open to the possibilities of God's redemption in unusual circumstances also inform faith and practice. Faith has as much to do with watching and waiting as it does with studying and praying. And sometimes action, not prayer, is the answer to a need!

Likewise, God's ways are not easily discovered. And sometimes our own religious traditions and observances—no matter how well meaning—can lead us away from God's gracious purposes.

This story is a reminder that, ultimately, God's redemptive work is accomplished in and through people—not through dormant piety or theological beliefs. As the Talmud says, "If you save one life, it is as if you had saved an entire world." Another truth is equally valid: "God has no hands but our hands."

~

The Voice
(Hindu)

A disciple came to learn at the feet of his guru. The guru told him, "God has many names, and one of these is Rama. If you look for God in all things, you will find safety wherever you go." The disciple departed and at once began to chant, "Rama, Rama," wherever he went.

One day he came to a village where a wild elephant was on the loose. As the disciple approached, the people of the village ran to him and warned him that the elephant had been heard nearby. "I am not worried," the disciple said. "As long as I see God in all things, I will not be harmed." The villagers, however, persisted with their warnings, but the disciple would not listen. "The elephant is God, I am God, and all about me is God—so why should I be frightened?" the disciple said. And with that word, he walked ahead into the village.

Sure enough, there was a mad elephant in the middle of the street. And naturally, when the elephant saw the man, he charged at him. "I am God and you are God," the disciple continued to chant. But even as the villagers cried out to help the disciple, the elephant picked him up and tossed him to the side of the road, nearly killing him.

Weeks later, after recovering from his injuries, the dazed disciple returned to his guru with this harrowing tale and a complaint. "You told me that if I saw God in all things I would be safe. But look what has happened to me!" the disciple exclaimed.

"Oh, foolish disciple," the guru replied. "You were right to see God in yourself and in the elephant. But how could you fail to hear the warning of God in the voice of the villagers?"

• • •

Faith may influence our decisions, but not at the expense of common sense. Furthermore, if one is going to trust in the protection of God, it is best not to jump from a tall building without a parachute.

Nearly every religion has certain theological perspectives or beliefs that are considered sacrosanct—much like the sacred cows that one cannot touch, even if they are in the middle of the road. But over time, religions also learn to challenge these accepted beliefs—if not in a theological fashion, at least in an offhanded or humorous way.

Here, one of the basic theological foundations of Hinduism—that the divine (or God, Rama) can be found and cherished in all things—is dealt a blow by a mad elephant. Rama may indeed be found in the elephant, as the guru suggests, but that does not mean that Rama can be ignored elsewhere. The premise must be carried forth to its logical conclusion to have validity.

Another way to look at this truth is to consider that people have a tendency to demonize those of other religious persuasions. But if God is everywhere, and near the person who professes faith, that person should also be able to see and hear God in those who are different. Likewise, those who ignore the wisdom of others run the risk of being destroyed by their own narrow perceptions of God.

A Good Harvest
(A parable of Jesus)

A farmer went out to scatter seed on the ground, and as he cast the seeds, some fell on a path, and the birds devoured them. Other seeds fell in a rocky place, and the seeds germinated quickly. But since the soil was not deep and they had no root, they withered away quickly when the sun rose and scorched them. Still other seeds fell into the thorns. But the thorns grew up and choked the seeds, so they were unable to get nourishment. And other seeds fell upon good, rich soil and brought forth an abundant harvest: thirty bushels to the acre, or sixty, and sometimes a hundred.

•　　•　　•

Frequently, in the New Testament gospels, an explanation follows a parable of Jesus. Here, Jesus supplies the interpretation to his disciples. "Those who hear the word of the kingdom, but allow the evil one to steal what is sown in the heart, are like those seeds which fell upon the path. Likewise, the seed sown upon the rocky ground is like one who hears the word and receives it immediately in joy; yet, because this person has no root, this one endures for a time, but falls away when trouble or hardships arise. And the seed that fell among the thorns? This is like the one who hears the word, but becomes lost in the cares of life and the desire for riches, and ends up with nothing. But as for the seed sown on the rich soil—this is the one who hears the word and understands it, and goes forth to bear much fruit for the kingdom."

In the gospels, the preface to this explanation is also worthy of note. As with many stories of Jesus, his followers did not understand the meaning. And so their question: "What does this mean?" was also an act of faith.

In this day when many people take stories literally, it is comforting to know that Jesus made it clear he was teaching in metaphors. Truth is rarely transparent. Meaning is derived from the experience of living in communion and community with God.

❧

The Fallen Traveler
(Christian)

Years ago there was a Buddhist monk named Sadhu who became a convert to the Christian faith. One day he was traveling in the mountains with another monk when a violent snowstorm descended, threatening to obscure the path that would lead them to shelter.

As they walked, suddenly they heard the sound of a man calling out for help. Rushing to the edge of a steep precipice,

Sadhu and the monk discovered a fellow traveler who had fallen from the path, lying injured below. When Sadhu stepped away from the path to help, the monk said, "Leave the man there."

"But why?" asked Sadhu.

"It is his fate," the monk pointed out. "He was destined to fall from the path and die."

"Whether it is his fate or not, I do not know," Sadhu replied. "But my Master says that when I see a brother in need, I must go to him."

At once Sadhu headed down the precipice, but the monk journeyed on, eager to get to the shelter farther down the path. Sadhu found the man, cared for his wounds, and helped him to stand. Together the two men emerged from the rocks and found the path again, the snow growing deeper with each step.

Many yards down the path they encountered the monk. He had lost his way, fallen on some rocks, and frozen to death.

"Who knows," said Sadhu, "whether by fate or the will of God we may save our own lives by helping each other."

•   •   •

The faith we live is far more important than the faith we profess. This is the heart of all true religion.

Here is a parable that attempts to define the limits of fate by demonstrating a relationship between good work and deliverance. Life, of course, has elements of chance and good/bad fortune, but that does not mean that circumstances define one's life. Rather, help can be rendered, decisions can be made, and choices can be exercised—and through these choices, the world can be changed.

The Quietness of Faith
(Hassidic)

The rabbi had become exhausted by the people's many questions. Exasperated by his people's inability to think for themselves, the rabbi set up a booth with a sign: "Any Two Questions Answered for $100."

The first day, one of the wealthiest men in the congregation showed up. He paid his money and then asked, "Rabbi,
isn't one hundred dollars rather a lot for the answers to two
questions?"

"Yes," said the rabbi. "And what is your second question?"

•   •   •

Any religious leader will understand the truths here. Most often,
it's much better to work things out in the quietness of faith and
struggle rather than in the certitude of pat answers. Answers
aren't always comforting.

It is also a case of human nature that people have looked to
religious leaders for answers for centuries. But leaders grow
weary of questions that deviate from the center of faith, or that
border on the trivial or mundane.

In Jewish tradition, Moses was the first to decry the inces-
sant complaints and questioning of the people, asking God, "Why
don't you let me die, so that I can be relieved of their misery?"
Anyone who has ever tried to lead a people of faith can identify
with this feeling. Fortunately, there are parables such as this one,
which help to alleviate some of the misery through laughter.

The Best Questions
(Christian)

There was a monk who would never give anyone advice—just
questions. If anyone came to him for wisdom, he would always
answer with a question. This style, however, was often quite
helpful.

One day Father Theophane approached the monk and said,
"I'm here on retreat, and I was wondering: could you give me
a question to ponder?"

The monk thought for a moment and then responded,
"My question for you is this: what do they need?"

Father Theophane went away disappointed, but a few
hours later returned to the monk for clarification. "Perhaps

I didn't make myself clear before," he said. "I'm here to work on my own spiritual life, not to reflect upon my calling as a priest. Could you possibly give me a question to ponder along these lines?"

"In that case," the monk said, "the question would be: what do they *really* need?"

· · ·

Spiritual matters are not always easy to discuss—much less contemplate. Sometimes our questions have a far greater significance than answers. Perhaps it is not the knowing that produces faith, but the doubts and uncertainties.

So often, we become aware of God through searching, by pondering life's questions and difficulties through new eyes. There is more of the childlike in our questions than we realize, and perhaps that is why so many spiritual leaders chose to tell stories or ask questions rather than to provide straightforward answers. Without imagination, faith dries up.

The best questions are always those that defy easy answers, enticing us to seek rather than sit.

A Piece of Truth
(Buddhist)

Mara, the Buddhist god of ignorance and evil, was passing through a village one day with his entourage when he saw a man walking down the road in deep meditation. Suddenly the man's eyes lit up as he leaned over and picked up an object.

Mara's entourage asked, "What did the man find on the ground?"

"A piece of truth," Mara explained.

"How awful! Doesn't this bother you when people discover a piece of truth, O evil one?"

"No," Mara replied. "Soon after this they usually make a belief out of it."

· · ·

Exactly what is faith? Is faith a belief, a creed, or a system of practices that one adheres to?

This parable suggests otherwise. Here the idea is put forth that truth is the ultimate goal of faith—but faith runs the risk of being destroyed as soon as belief, creed, or tradition diminishes it. Of course, as the story suggests, this is a difficulty. People of all faiths have a tendency to present or protect truth in imperfect ways. The danger is that form can become more important than function, and truth can be hidden by language, or meaning, or culture. In the end, the greatest danger is that truth is rarely offered to those outside a faith in a spirit of love.

This story also suggests that some people may hold others hostage—in a theological sense—demanding that others use the same words or feelings to express their faith. When this happens, one group may deem another group of people to be inferior. Even people of the same faith can hold some hostage to these extremes.

The parable offers us a gentle reminder that truth, in and of itself, is never enough. All truth must be accompanied by love and understanding—which are the greatest measures of faith.

The Good Neighbor
(A parable of Jesus)

A scholar of religious law once asked Jesus, "Who is my neighbor?"

Jesus replied with this story.

"A man going on a journey fell among robbers, who stripped him of his clothing, beat him, and left him for dead along the side of the road. By chance, a priest was traveling that way. But when he saw the man lying wounded along the road, he passed by on the other side. Likewise, a religious scholar came by, but he also passed on the other side.

"Finally, a man regarded as a pagan was traveling that day. When he saw the man lying wounded, he went to him, anointed and bound his wounds, set him on his animal, and took him to a nearby inn. He told the innkeeper, 'Please care for this man. And when I return, I will pay you for your expenses.'"

Then Jesus asked the scholar, "Which of these three, do you think, was a neighbor to the man who fell among the robbers?"

The scholar replied, "The one who showed mercy."

•   •   •

In every religion, there are deeply embedded traditions and beliefs. But as this parable points out, it is often difficult for adherents to distinguish between the inner essence of a living faith and the outward display of a doctrine. Faith binds us closer to God and neighbor, while doctrines and beliefs (particularly as they inform us about the "proper" way of relating to others) can often drive us away from God's work and the needs of the world. Living faith, however small, is always greater than blind adherence to creeds.

This parable is also regarded as one of the greatest teachings of Jesus. As was common among Jewish teachers of the first century, Jesus was a rabbinic storyteller, a master of narrative and metaphor. This story probes to the heart of our attitudes toward others—particularly those outside our faith tradition— and calls us to find the neighbor in everyone, or in every need, we encounter.

Miraculous Powers
(Sufi)

A disciple approached a renowned Sufi and said, "I know someone who can walk on water." The Sufi replied, "So what? That's simple. A frog and a mosquito can also walk on water."

"But I know another man who can fly," the disciple boasted.

"Nothing special," answered the Sufi. "Insects and birds can also fly."

Finally the disciple said, "I know a man who can travel from one city to another in an instant."

"Ah, but so can Satan," answered the Sufi. "None of the abilities you have mentioned are of any value. A true human being is one who can interact with people and yet remember God in all things."

•   •   •

Trust in God is the center of faith. Life offers many rich experiences and rewarding gifts, but without God, we forget the source of all good things.

This Sufi masterpiece is reminiscent of the plagues of Egypt, and the temptations of Jesus in the wilderness. Although there are many signs and wonders, the story demonstrates that not all miracles and signs are from God. Some wonders are natural occurrences; others are simply bogus.

One who trusts in God does not need miracles to validate his or her faith. Faith is enough in itself, and is its own reward.

The true miracle, however, is when one learns to live well—practicing generosity of spirit, helpfulness, and kindness, and is open to the work and will of God. Although people have always been drawn to the miraculous, to signs and wonders, it is the faithful who serve, sacrifice, and labor for others who are the true miracles in our midst.

Small Discoveries
(Parables of Jesus)

The kingdom of heaven is like a grain of mustard seed planted in the ground. This seed is the smallest of all, but when it grows and matures, it becomes larger than any other plant in the garden. Eventually it becomes a tree—large enough for the birds of the air to roost in and make their nests.

The kingdom of heaven is also like a treasure buried in a field. Someone comes by, finds the treasure, and buries it again.

In great joy, this person goes out and sells everything in order to buy that field and claim the treasure.

•　　•　　•

The simplicity of these parables points to the life-changing power of faith, and the joy that accompanies the realization that God's grace is sufficient in life. Faith has the power to transform and to make new—and the object of faith, ultimately, is God alone.

Faith also has the ability to expand our world and to broaden our relationships. Like the tiny mustard seed that grows into a magnificent tree, even a bit of faith can produce tremendous results in a person's life. Faith has the power to bring others into the sanctuary of God's love.

Like the treasure in the field, faith also offers new possibilities. Sometimes risk is necessary to reap the reward, but faith is the ability to see beneath the surface of a situation and envision a greater outcome. As in all walks of life, the true visionaries of our time are people of faith—those who can see a bit further, a bit more clearly, those who can see the larger picture. When this vision is applied to the things of God, the result is that the kingdom of heaven comes a little nearer to earth.

The Religious Fanatic
(Sufi)

There once was a convert who had a reputation for being a religious fanatic. Over time, he became known for his angry attacks on nonbelievers.

One day, a wise teacher asked him, "Why are you such a fanatic with your faith?"

The convert explained, "For years I served the devil. Now I serve God. I have dedicated my life to exposing the wrong beliefs of others, demonstrating how their doctrines are false, and that anything that is not of the true faith is misleading and blasphemous. This mission is a full-time job for me."

The teacher asked him, "But do you try to put yourself in your opponents' positions, and try to understand their beliefs, before you attack them?"

"Certainly," the convert replied. "In fact, I have studied such false beliefs thoroughly in order to make my arguments all the more sound. By study, I discover the weaknesses and expose them to the light of my truths!"

Suddenly the wise teacher exploded into a tirade, pointed his finger at the convert, and began calling the man names until the convert backed away and begged him to stop.

Afterwards, the teacher explained. "In order to put yourself in the place of others, it is not enough to know what they believe. You must also know what they feel. Only when you understand people in this way will you be a true servant of the truth."

•   •   •

Among the religions of the world, intolerance and anger toward those of other faiths or beliefs can have devastating consequences. One does not have to agree with another person to feel empathy and love for that person. Intellectual and religious knowledge alone does not make one faithful and wise to the truths of God. Compassion is greater in the eyes of God than condemnation of others' beliefs.

Here the ancient Native American proverb still applies: Do not judge another person until you have walked a day in his moccasins.

Knowing what another person believes never provides a full and accurate snapshot of that person's life. In fact, we rarely come to know another person fully without emotional attachment. We may know how a person thinks, but may have no idea what makes that person laugh or cry.

In many instances, it is not the pagan who needs to be converted or changed, but the one who is religious.

The Meaning of Heaven and Hell
(Zen Buddhist)

A mighty samurai warrior once went to see a little old monk and demanded in a threatening voice, "Teach me about heaven and hell!"

The little old monk looked at this mountain of man and said, "Teach you about heaven and hell, will I? Not on your life. Why, look at you! You are dirty. You smell. You have a rusted sword. You're a disgrace to the samurai class. Get out of here! I can't stand the sight of you!"

Enraged, the samurai raised his sword to smite the monk. But as he was getting ready to strike, the monk bowed his head and said in a soft voice, "That is hell."

Overcome with compassion and repentance for his anger, the samurai lowered his weapon. After a moment of silence, the monk raised his head and noted the peaceful face of the grateful samurai.

"That is heaven," the monk said.

•   •   •

Imagery and metaphor for heaven and hell can be found in almost all religions. While particular beliefs about the afterlife may differ, there is a common element in each. Heaven has to do with the things of God—including nearness to God and a sense of completeness and joy—while hell is often described or thought of as separation from God, and a sense of incompleteness and loss.

In some belief systems, these realities are yet to come. In others, these realities are descriptions of the life now lived, and the promise of what the world could be.

In Buddhism, Zen has achieved a greater level of acceptance and appeal in Western societies than the classical form of Buddhism. Zen first came to Japan in the mid-twelfth century, when a monk named Eisai returned from China with the new philosophical approach. Unlike its more classical counterpart—which emphasized ritual—Zen was fiercely demanding, emphasizing personal effort and offering enlightenment rather than heaven itself. For these reasons, among others, Zen did not initially meet with an enthusiastic welcome.

However, in time, Zen Buddhism developed its own meditative rituals, arts, and letters. Among Zen's abundant literature are parables of enlightenment and humor.

The parable of the monk and the samurai is a classic tale, told in Zen style. Hell, as the parable suggests, is the path of anger and destruction. Heaven, on the other hand, is peace and tranquility—true enlightenment.

The Lunatic
(Hindu)

A holy man fell into a state of ecstasy and would speak to no one. Because of this, the villagers regarded him as a lunatic. One day he sat down on the street next to a dog and began to eat. The holy man would take a bite, and then give a bite to the dog. They shared the food like old friends.

When the villagers began to laugh at him, he silenced them by saying, "Why do you laugh? Vishnu is seated next to Vishnu. Vishnu is feeding Vishnu. Why do you laugh, O Vishnu? Whatever is, is Vishnu."

• • •

According to the Hindu faith, God is all, and all is God. There is nothing that God does not touch, and nothing that one can touch that is not God. Seeing goodness and beauty in all things produces some strange paradoxes. Living in the conviction that God is all and in all would indeed broaden the heart to love what others might reject.

The Banquet of Opportunity
(Jewish)

Once there was a rich man who wanted to have a banquet. He invited all his friends, especially those of high standing, and purchased the finest foods and the most exotic drinks. On the night before the festivities, he dreamed that his moment of redemption would come during the banquet, and so he was anxious to be on his guard, lest he miss the moment when God would draw near to him.

The next evening, during the banquet, he made every effort to talk with each guest, to make certain that everyone was enjoying the festivities. Late in the evening, as the banquet was drawing to a close, one of the host's best friends came to the party with a young boy and girl. The two young people spent the evening dancing together and talking to the other guests.

Now the host was at first amused by these two, but he grew weary of their youthful zest and energy. Before the party came to a close, the young man and woman approached the host and announced that they would like to be married. The host turned them away, insisting that they were not right for each other, and that they were too young to marry. Furthermore, he asked them to leave the banquet.

That night, the rich man had another dream. God told him, "If you had only approved the marriage of the young man and woman your redemption would have come. I was the One who sent them to you. The boy and girl were none other than the angels Michael and Gabriel."

•   •   •

Opportunities for redemption and service are never far off. God does not abide in the ethereal beyond, but in the here and now. Therefore, it is important to watch for moments of divine incarnation, to be attentive to new circumstances, and to treat others with respect. One can never know when God might show up.

Where Is the Lord?
(Sufi)

A respected worshipper made his first pilgrimage to Mecca. Weary from his travels, he lay down on the ground to sleep, but was soon awakened by an irate Muslim who said, "The time has come for everyone to bow their heads toward Mecca. But you have your feet pointed toward the Lord."

The man opened his eyes slightly, and then instructed the Muslim to adjust his feet in a direction where they would not point to the Lord.

• • •

Where is God? Some say in heaven. Some maintain that God abides in holy places. Some believe that God dwells in the hearts of the faithful. Others insist that God is everywhere—present and accessible to all.

Likewise, some envision faith as a wall—a barrier that keeps the wrong people out. Others see faith as a doorway—an opening through which people can enter.

This little parable insists that, wherever one finds God, there is a spirit of peace.

The Value of Religion
(Jewish)

A skeptic came to the rabbi with questions. "What good is religion?" the skeptic asked. "There is so much trouble and misery in the world despite hundreds of years of teaching about goodness, faith, and loving one's neighbor. If religion were true, wouldn't it make sense that the world would be a better place?"

The rabbi did not answer right away. But when he spied a little boy who was filthy, he said, "Take a look at that little boy. He is dirty. Yet you and I both know that soap will make him clean. Still, he is dirty. Does this mean that soap is useless?"

"But Rabbi," the skeptic observed, "soap is of no value unless it is used."

"Exactly," said the rabbi. "So it is with religion. It is of no value unless it is applied and used."

•   •   •

What is faith? Is it a system of belief, a declaration or a doctrine, a creed to which one adheres? Or is faith an activity, the manner in which one lives in relationship to others and to God?

As this beautiful parable demonstrates, no amount of official teaching or doctrine will have a long-lasting impact in the world. A religion is only as good as the daily practice and witness of the ones who profess it. One can believe many things, yet still lack faith. And one can profess a belief in God, yet still hate others.

The core teaching of all faith is service, care for the weak, and living an exemplary life as an offering to God. Everything else is commentary.

Salvation Has Come
(Hindu)

In order to offer salvation, the God Shiva and his wife, the Goddess Parvati, decided to visit earth disguised as a holy man and his disciple. Soon it became known that this holy man and his disciple could not only tell a person's past, but could also prophesy the future. Great crowds gathered.

One man approached and said, "Please tell me when I will obtain my salvation. I am most devout. In the winter I meditate while submerged in ice water. In the summer I meditate sitting in a ring of fire. For years I have eaten only a single meal of fruit and milk each day."

The holy man said, "Indeed you are most devout. If you continue to practice such devotion you will obtain salvation after three births."

The man, upon hearing this, went away disappointed. He returned to his friends muttering, "Still three births."

Others then came forward asking the same question. Each pointed out the depth of his devotion, the hardships he had endured to subdue the body, the sacrifices made. Afterwards, each received an answer from the holy man. Some were given salvation after five births, others seven, or ten, or twenty. Each went away disappointed.

Finally, a man came forward who was thin and ugly. He was a hermit who had never spent a single day in meditation or prayer. He asked, "And what about me? I must confess that I have spent no time in prayer. But I do love God's creation. I am kind to others. Is it possible for me to receive salvation?"

The holy man said, "If you go on loving God in this way, perhaps after a thousand births, you, too, may find salvation."

The hermit's eyes lit up and he began to dance around in joy. "I can get salvation! I can get salvation!" Suddenly, as he danced, his body became a flame. Likewise, Shiva's body burst into fire, and so did Parvati's. These three flames joined together and ascended into heaven.

•   •   •

Every religion has its traditions and paradoxes. Here, faith is defined as a state of innocence, joy, and complete surrender. Pride and ego get in the way. Jesus spoke of this state when he said, "Unless you become as children, you cannot enter the kingdom." Zen Buddhism speaks of this state as "the beginner's mind."

No matter what our faith, the standard practices and expectations of believers is a confusing state of affairs. We want a faith neatly packaged, but what we get is a faith-struggle in an ever-changing world. Simplicity matters. Too many practices and traditions make a faith dull and lifeless.

Salvation is surrender and the supreme joy of being at peace with God.

The Man Who Walked on Water
(Hindu)

A man wanted to walk across the sea. So a holy man wrote the name of God on a leaf, tied it inside the man's sash, and told him, "Do not be afraid. Have faith and you will walk on the water. One thing, however: the moment you lose faith, you will drown."

The man began his journey across the sea, walking on top of the water. But miles beyond the shore, he began to wonder what the holy man had tucked inside his sash. He removed his garment and found a single leaf with the word RAMA written on it. "What is this?" the man thought. "Just the name of God."

Immediately doubt entered his mind and he began to sink.

•　　•　　•

Faith, in part, is the ability to focus. When we look away from the object of devotion—namely, God—we lose our way. In most cultures, the ocean represents the chaotic elements of the world—that which we cannot control. Faith, then, keeps a person above the chaos and enables one to walk unharmed.

It is important to remember that distractions abound. There are many enticements, even religious ones, that can destroy a fragile faith.

A Jar of Meal
(Gospel of Thomas)

Jesus said, "The kingdom of God is like a woman carrying a jar of meal. As she was walking along the road, but was still a long distance from home, the handle of the jar broke and the meal began pouring out along the roadside. But she did not realize the meal was spilling out behind her as she walked along. When she arrived at her house and set the jar down, she was shocked to find that the jar was empty."

•   •   •

In 1945, archaeologists discovered a collection of ancient manuscripts in Nag Hammadi, Egypt. These first-century Christian documents became known as the Nag Hammadi library, and among them was a Gnostic gospel consisting of the teachings of Jesus. Some of these teachings are included in the New Testament gospels, but there are also parables and sayings found only in this ancient text.

This unique parable is fascinating because it provokes several questions about the life of faith. As the parable seems to suggest, faith is a provision that one gives away and uses through the journey of life. The goal is to arrive at the end of the journey having emptied oneself in the process. We are not always aware of this emptying as we move through life, but the result is always a surprise.

Like many parables of its kind, this tale is an invitation to believe in what one cannot see, and to share in the mystery of God's work. God provides more than enough to complete the journey. What we do with these gifts is up to us.

3

Hope Springs Eternal

*All human wisdom is summed up
in two words—wait and hope.*

—Alexandre Dumas

Hope can take many forms. Sometimes hope comes to us in words of comfort or expressions of care. At other times hope is the mere presence of another person during a crisis or moment of sorrow. And there are circumstances when we receive hope through unexpected joy.

Taken as a whole, the parables in this chapter will deliver hope from many vantage points and from a variety of traditions. Some will provide comfort, others a respite through laughter. But the careful reader will find a source of hope in a world that is filled with conflict and challenge.

Among the many stories of the Buddha, there is a simple parable that embodies the nature of hope.

A fellow had fallen into a deep pit, clinging to a vine for safety. After a time, naturally, his arms began to grow tired, and it was at this point he also noticed that two mice were gnawing at the vine. Looking below, he realized that if the vine broke, he would fall into the pit of vipers.

Suddenly, just above his head, he noticed a small beehive. Every few seconds, a small dot of honey would drip from the hive. Upon seeing this, the man stuck out his tongue and tasted the sweet honey, forgetting all his troubles.

Hope, for lack of a better analogy, is like honey in a bitter world. Hope is the sweetness that comes to us through our troubles, allowing us, for a time at least, to forget our hardships and to take heart.

Perhaps these parables might sweeten your life a bit and set you on a path leading to renewal and strength.

A Kind Word
(Desert Fathers)

Two old men had lived together for many years and had never had an argument. But at last one of them said, "Let's at least attempt to have a disagreement like normal people." The other replied, "I don't even know how an argument begins."

Holding a brick in his hands, the first man said, "See this brick. The argument will work like this. I will place it in the middle, between us. I will say it is mine; you say it is yours. Then we have an argument."

So they placed the brick in the middle and the first man said, "This is my brick!"

The second said, "No, it's mine!"

Then the first responded, "I know it's yours. Please take it."

So they went away, unable to argue with each other.

•   •   •

The Desert Fathers represent an eclectic Christian tradition that began in the third century, when groups of Christians began leaving the church in Egypt to live an ascetic life in the desert. These hermits believed the church had adapted to the prevailing culture and had grown to ignore the simple commands of Jesus to sell possessions, to give to the poor, and to follow Jesus's example of a life of simple humility.

These followers lived in caves, huts, or simple brick-and-mortar cells, devoid of comforts. In addition to living as simply as possible, these hermits sometimes deprived themselves of food and water, and worked long hours, supporting themselves by weaving mats. Their efforts eventually resulted in a golden age of "Desert Father" wisdom traditions, with an abundance of parables and teachings that were passed along from one generation to the next.

Gradually, as more Christians moved to the desert, leaders were selected. These became, in time, the abbots who led the monastic movement that began to take shape in the fifth and sixth centuries.

This parable reminds us of the pettiness that pervades most disagreements and the hope that can be wrought through cooperation and gentleness. As one biblical proverb states, "A kind word turns away wrath."

One observation about arguments is that the majority could be avoided altogether. Many arguments are drawn out because one or both parties are unwilling to admit to being wrong, or to concede that, at the very least, there might be some validity on the other side. Other arguments continue because one or both parties believe there is something of greater value at stake, and there is no willingness to compromise. Still others are perpetuated because one or both parties cannot see the pettiness of the argument itself. Sometimes, it is difficult, as they say, to see the forest for the trees.

This parable points out the futility of entrenched disagreements and offers the way of peace, compromise, and reconciliation as a noble alternative.

The Last-Minute Pardon
(African)

One day a man said to his wife, "I want you to braid my hair into four parts." His wife did this, and then the man sat under a tree and invited the neighbors to come and guess what each of the four parts represented. Each neighbor was invited to bring a calf, and the one who could guess correctly would receive the calves as a prize. The man told his wife what the parts represented: "The first braid is: a wife is a stranger.

The second braid is: a dog is a loyal friend. The third braid is: a half-brother is a stranger. And the fourth braid is: a brother-in-law is a loyal friend." Then he sat beneath the tree for days as people from miles around came to guess.

Now, because the man was doing no work, the government officials became very suspicious of him. They secretly decided that the man should be hanged if anyone guessed the secret to his riddle. Day after day people came with their calves, but no one guessed correctly.

One day the man's wife was talking to a nephew when the nephew asked, "Why does uncle sit under the tree all day and do nothing? What is so important about this game?" Unable to keep the secret any longer, the man's wife told the nephew the answer to the riddle.

The next day the nephew came to his uncle and asked, "May I guess?"

"Certainly," the uncle said.

And the nephew proceeded to spout off the answer to the riddle.

However, as soon as the government officials saw this, they took the man away to be executed. But the man begged, "Please do not kill me before I can say good-bye to my family."

Feeling pity for the man, the government officials allowed him to return home for one day, though under heavy guard. When the man spoke to his wife, however, she was unsympathetic. "Who told you to do such a stupid thing?" she said.

"Well, at least give me a glass of milk before I die," the man pleaded.

"No!" his wife answered. "Why should I waste good milk on a man who is already dead?"

The man, heavyhearted and alone, went out to the barn to weep. As he cried, his dogs grew protective of their master and rushed upon the guards, killing two of them. The other guards, however, managed to shackle the man and cart him away to be executed.

Now on the way back to prison, the man's half-brother met him on the road. "Is it true, brother, that they are going to kill you?" the half-brother asked.

"Yes," the man replied.

"Well, then," the half-brother replied, "it would be a terrible thing to waste such a fine robe. Why don't you give it to me so that I can get some use from it, and I, in return, will give you this tattered robe to die in."

Taken aback by his half-brother's callousness, the man continued on his journey to the gallows, but sent word to his sister's family, saying, "I am going to be executed. Would someone from your family please come to see me before I die?"

The next day, just before the execution, the man's brother-in-law showed up at the prison. "Don't kill this man!" the brother-in-law pleaded with the government officials. "If you must take a life, take mine! I will die in his place! If you do not listen, something terrible will happen to you all."

At this word the officials gathered together to discuss the curious turn of events. They approached the man and asked, "Why did you play such a silly game in the first place?"

The man answered, "I wanted to prove what has just happened! I gave the secret to my wife and she betrayed me, then she gave me no comfort when I was about to die. My dogs were loyal and tried to protect me from the officials. My half-brother desired my robe, even when I was on my way to the gallows. And now my brother-in-law has come, willing to die for me. This is what I wanted to prove through the riddle."

Naturally, the officials understood what the man was talking about and decided to release him. He returned to his home a happy and free man.

•   •   •

This tale reveals the strange twists of fate that can turn a harmless joke into a life-and-death situation. Within the story, however, there is an affirmation that every cloud can have a silver lining. Often the greatest source of hope is our ability to experience joy in the midst of anguish.

Many African parables use the story itself to prove a point mentioned within the story. The four parts of the riddle are meant to teach truths about society and observations about life, but they are offered within the context of a zany tale.

Implied in the parable is that the wise person always has hope of prevailing over his or her oppressors. There is no need to give up, as life has a way of presenting unexpected opportunities.

A Peace of Mind
(Taoist)

Lao Tan died, and Ch'in Shih went to his funeral, wailing three times before he left. Afterward, Lao Tan's disciples asked, "Weren't you a friend of the master?"

"Yes," Ch'in Shih answered.

"Then how can you mourn him so weakly?" they asked.

"This is life," Ch'in Shih replied. "But when I went to the funeral I saw the old weeping for him in the way parents weep for their children when they die, and I saw the young weeping for him in the way children weep for their parents when they die. But when the master was born, it was his time. And when he died, he went along. If you are at peace with your time and seek to live in harmony with each other, sadness and happiness cannot affect you."

• • •

A basic teaching of Taoism is that one can arrive at an inner peace, thereby learning to accept the unpredictable forces of life and death. This simple parable from *Chuang-tzu* seeks to teach this by demonstrating that our actions and our words can produce a peace of mind and a harmony with others, rather than produce feelings of loss and separation. When we learn to accept this peace, there is no longer any need for social pretense and practice. Finding this inner peace and this harmony with others brings us closer to enlightenment.

In addition, many Taoist parables demonstrate two subtle truths inherent in Western religious thought—that one cannot control life or the future, and if one attempts to understand why things happen as they do, there are no answers.

Sometimes, hope rests in learning how to be, rather than attempting to become. There are many circumstances that cannot be changed, no matter how much effort is put forth. Learning how to be at peace with this truth brings us one step closer to enlightenment.

Hoping for Forgiveness
(Desert Fathers)

There were three old men who came to visit the teacher. One of these men had a bad reputation and was not liked by his companions. The first man said to the teacher, "Father, make me a fishing net."

"I will not make you one," the teacher said.

The second man came to the teacher with the same request, "Father, make me a fishing net."

Again, the reply was the same. "I will not make you one."

Finally, the fellow with the bad reputation said, "Please, Father, make me a fishing net. That way I will have something to remember you by."

"For you I will make one," the teacher said.

Later, when the two followers were alone with their teacher, they asked him, "Why was it that you wouldn't make a fishing net for either of us, yet you made one for that troublemaker whom no one can tolerate?"

The teacher replied, "When I told you I wouldn't make you a fishing net, you were not disappointed in me, since you assumed I had no time. But if I had not made a net for him, he would have said, 'The teacher has surely heard about my sin, and that is why he will not make me a fishing net.' And so this would have been a rift in our relationship. But by making him a net, I have cheered his soul, and he will not be overcome with grief. Often, we must make special rules for those whom we regard as weaker."

•   •   •

This parable holds out the hope of forgiveness for those who may feel ostracized from the community. The story is not exclusively for religious communities, but may hold practical promise for helping us to understand the relationship between generosity and acceptance. Sometimes, we have the most difficulty forgiving ourselves. Receiving care from others can be a healing force.

The real difficulty, however, as this parable demonstrates, emerges when feelings of moral superiority surface. The story reminds us that we must look within and understand our need for help before we can offer assistance to another.

The Location of Paradise
(Hassidic)

The rabbi once had a dream of paradise. He entered by being dunked in a deep well, and when he came out, he saw only a few saints sitting at tables and studying Torah. The rabbi asked the accompanying angel, "Is this all there is to paradise?"

The angel answered, "You seem to think that the saints are in paradise. But you have it backwards. Paradise is in the saints!"

• • •

So often our hope is tied up in ethereal ideas that never materialize. We can grow despondent when grand and lofty ideas do not come to fruition.

Here is a little story that reminds us to keep our feet on the ground. If God is present, then God is present in people. If we want heaven, it is best to begin the search close to home.

All the grandest hopes of the human race—hope for peace, justice, and mercy—can never be realized until we see the image of God in one another.

The Journey of Togetherness
(Hassidic)

A man went into the woods to hunt, but lost his way. For days he wandered in the forest, disoriented and confused, desperately trying to find his way out.

After some time, he saw another man approaching in the distance. His hopes soared. *At last,* he thought to himself, *a person who knows how to get out of this forest.*

When they met, he asked the man, "My brother, can you tell me the way out of this forest? I have been wandering for days, but have been unable to find the way."

The other fellow answered, "Brother, I do not know the way out either. I, too, have been wandering about these woods for days. But this much I can tell you—do not go the way that I have gone. I know for certain that it does not lead out. Let us journey on together. Perhaps, side by side, we can figure a way out."

●   ●   ●

Here we discover that feelings of hopelessness are more likely to emerge when there is isolation and individualism. These feelings are all the more acute in the modern world, where life itself can become a forest—an entanglement of commitments, crowded calendars, and infatuation with achievement.

When we learn to grow beyond our problems, we discover sources of healing and renewal. As Winston Churchill once pointed out: "We make a living by what we get. We build a life by what we give."

There is hope when we realize that we are not alone in our struggles. We have a need to help others. And there are times when we need to receive help.

Another summary of this parable may be found in this adage: Two heads are better than one.

Bound Together
(Aesop)

A father had four sons who were always arguing. One day he decided to teach them a lesson. He gathered four sticks and tied them together with twine.

Later, the father gathered his sons together and asked them to break the sticks. Each tried, but none of the sons was able to do it.

Next the father untied the bundle and gave each of the sons a single stick. These they broke without any trouble.

"You see," the father said, "when you are bound together, you are strong. But when you are divided, you are weak."

•   •   •

Aesop is, no doubt, the most well-known of the Greek moralists. His parables—whether written by Aesop or collected by him—have been read in homes, taught in schools, and recited at bedtime. Many of the stories have worked their way into our cultural psyche as social lessons and observations.

This simple parable points to the truth of strength through agreement. When there is unity, there is power. But division casts doubt and aspersion on any achievement or relationship.

As the story illustrates, it is good to remember that alone we are weak. But when joined together with others in a common cause, we find strength.

The Rabbi's Daughters
(Jewish)

There was a rabbi who had three daughters. However, because the family was very poor, the daughters had but one dress among them—a dress that they took turns sharing. Whenever one daughter went into town, she would wear the dress and the other two would stay home.

Now, this poverty was very upsetting to the rabbi, and he prayed that God might alleviate their suffering. They had but crusts of bread to eat, and an old rooster that was hardly fit to cook.

One day a holy man came to visit the rabbi. He sat down at table and asked if he might have something to eat.

The rabbi brought him a few crusts of bread, then called out to his daughters, "Go get the rooster, take it to the butcher shop in town, and have it prepared for our guest."

The youngest of the daughters jumped up, put the dress on, tucked the rooster under her arm, and set off for town. Not far down the road, however, the rooster got loose and began to flap and flutter, trying to fly away. The girl ran after the bird, trying to catch it as it leaped over fields, scurried across roads, and bounded over a fence.

Eventually the girl managed to get her hands on the rooster, but when she grabbed it, her dress caught on the corner of the fence and was ripped from top to bottom. "Oh no!" she cried. "How will I be able to show myself in town in this condition? How will I be able to get the rooster to the butcher, and then home again in time for dinner?"

All of the spirit went out of her when she thought of her father sitting at home. A deep sadness swept over her and she sat by a tree and wept.

As evening approached, however, the sun's rays moved lower to the ground. Suddenly the girl caught a glimpse of something bright and sparkling beneath a nearby tree. She had heard stories of hidden treasure, but had never believed them. Forgetting her tears, she went to see for herself what this glittering was.

Sure enough, it was a golden treasure. Elated with her discovery, she gathered up the gold and headed toward home.

Meanwhile, the rabbi and the holy man sat at table, wondering where the youngest daughter could be. It was very late in the evening when the girl came through the door, carrying the gold.

The rabbi began to scold his daughter, assuming that she had stolen the treasure. But the holy man said, "Your daughter is not a thief. God has provided this gold as an answer to your prayers. The holy One, blessed be his name, always provides."

•   •   •

There is a saying that God watches over beggars and fools. Many Jewish stories celebrate this age-old tradition, but also point to God as the provider of all good things, especially in difficult times. No one, no matter how needy or poor, is unworthy of God's generosity.

Difficulties also have a way of magnifying problems. Small inconveniences can loom large when life is stretched to the limit. Losses mount. And then, when all seems hopeless, help arrives as something of a miracle. That is why, in most cultures, there are classic rags-to-riches stories—often ending with a divine twist. These stories remind us that all good things come from above.

Persistence Pays Off
(Parables of Jesus)

A man received an unexpected guest, so he went to a friend's house at midnight and began to knock on the door. "Open up," he said, "and give me some food. I have an unexpected guest and have nothing to feed him."

But the friend answered from behind the locked door, "Go away. Do not bother me. The door is already locked, my children are in bed, and I cannot give you anything."

The fellow continued to knock, however, until his friend rose from bed and gave him everything he asked for.

There was also a woman who had a matter of justice to settle before the judge. The judge, however, was unwilling to listen to her case.

Nevertheless, this woman continued to plead her cause before the judge until he grew weary of her and gave her everything she requested.

• • •

These insightful stories offer hope for those in need, and serve to remind us that prayer and persistence are key factors when asking God for help. Answers may not always come easily, or in a timely manner, but eventually the way becomes clear. Often, it is not in our time that prayers are answered, but in God's.

Jesus offered these parables when he was asked to explain prayer. They provide the hope that all things are possible with God, and that, in terms of human understanding, we can always take our needs to One who is greater.

These simple stories also challenge the classic notion of prayer as magic words or ritual. Simple expression is what God desires.

Consider the following similar Jewish parable that, at its heart, is about prayer.

The Singer
(Jewish)

There once lived a simple man who enjoyed offering his song to God. The trouble was, he could scarcely carry a tune. But, because the congregation could afford no better singer, this man was allowed to continue as the song leader.

After some years, however, the rabbi announced that the congregation had enough money to hire a well-known singer to lead the congregation. Everyone was pleased with this announcement and was glad to see the simple singer go.

One evening, some weeks later, an angel appeared to the rabbi and asked, "Where is the music that once rose up to God? There is no longer any sound of joy and thanksgiving coming from this place."

The rabbi quickly pointed out that in fact the congregation had recently hired a new singer, and his music was first rate.

"So that is the problem," said the angel. "The new singer offers his music for the praise of others, and thereby goes unheard by God. But the simple singer offered his music to God alone, and thereby made beautiful music in heaven."

A Circle of Light
(Sufi)

One evening Nasrudin was seen outside his house, rummaging on his hands and knees by lantern light. A friend came by and asked what he was doing.

"I'm looking for a lost key," said Nasrudin.

The friend got down on his hands and knees to help with the search. After some time the friend asked, "Where, exactly did you lose this key?"

Nasrudin answered, "I lost it in the house. But there is more light out here."

• • •

Here is another humorous parable about the Sufi master Nasrudin. Light is the key metaphor here. In life, sometimes it is not what we have lost that is most important, but what we hope to find that is transforming. We often lose one thing, but discover something new in the search.

The parable also points to another truth. We must leave behind the familiar and venture into the unknown in order to make new discoveries. Risk is necessary if we are to achieve new goals.

There are times in life when one is better off leaving behind the old to embrace the new. Although this is difficult, and may even seem silly, the payoff can be very rewarding.

The Banker and the Skeptic
(Jewish)

The great teacher Gamaliel was once asked to explain why people afflicted with disease are sometimes healed, even though they do not believe in God. The teacher told this story:

"There was a certain man of the city who enjoyed the complete trust of the people. This man was so respected and admired that everyone gave him their money without a witness present to oversee the transaction. Everyone, that is, except one fellow who trusted no one. This fellow always brought along a witness when he made his deposits.

"Now, it turned out that one day this distrusting fellow forgot to bring along a witness when he made his deposit with the banker. The banker's wife, hearing of this, tried to talk her husband into denying that this man had made the deposit, saying, 'Who will believe him? He trusts no one, and, besides, this could teach him a lesson.'

"But the banker answered, 'Why would I do this? Should I deny my principles for the sake of a few dollars? Why wouldn't I continue to be generous and trustworthy with regard to this man, and all the more so since he does not believe in me?!'"

•   •   •

This is one of the most famous parables attributed to Rabbi Gamaliel, who was a contemporary of both Jesus and the apostle Paul. In fact, Paul mentions Gamaliel as one of his teachers in the New Testament book of Acts (22:3). The rabbis of Jesus's day were the Pharisees of the Bible. These teachers believed that along with the written Torah God had also provided an oral tradition. These oral laws were later collected as the Talmud.

Gamaliel's parable offers the belief that all people—regardless of belief—have been blessed by God. God shows no favoritism based on belief. Rather, there is a wideness in God's mercy that encompasses the righteous and the unrighteous alike. Life itself is a gift. And, as Jesus himself taught, God provides blessings to all.

God's Banquet
(Gospel of Thomas)

Jesus said, "A man wanted to have a dinner for his friends. So he sent his servant to issue the necessary invitations. But the first friend said, 'I have a business matter to attend to this evening. I ask to be excused from the dinner.' A second friend said, 'I just bought a house and must take care of matters there for the day. I ask to be excused from the dinner.' Another friend said, 'I have a friend who is getting married and I am in charge of the banquet. I ask to be excused from the dinner.' A fourth responded, 'I just bought a farm and I am on my way to collect the rent. I will not be able to come, and therefore I ask to be excused from the dinner.'

"And so each refused the invitation.

"When the servant returned to the master, he said, 'All those you invited to the dinner have asked to be excused.'

"So the master said, 'Go into the street and bring back anyone you meet, so that they may enjoy my dinner.'"

•   •   •

Similar to the parable of the banquet found in the New Testament gospels, this story reminds us that God's grace reaches unexpected people and places. Even though some refuse the invitation to dine with the master, the host takes the initiative to fill the banquet table. The invitation is wide and embracing. Those left outside are often the first to enter.

There is a marvelous hope that, even in our inability to receive the hospitality of heaven, we might be counted among those who are invited at the last hour.

Snail's Pace
(Sufi)

The animals got together for an assembly and began to complain. "People are always taking things from us," said the monkey.

"They take my milk," said the cow.

"They take my eggs," said the hen.

"They take my flesh and call it bacon," said the pig.

"They kill me for my oil," said the whale.

Finally the snail came forward and spoke. "I have something people would take from me if they could," he said. "It is the one thing they want more than anything else: Time!"

• • •

This is a simple parable containing a majestic truth. The most valuable commodity you and I possess is time. We guard it, crave it, and enjoy it. Time may be given in equal measure to every person each day, but how one uses the gift is perhaps the greatest disparity in life. Some use time wisely; others foolishly.

Time, unlike other commodities, cannot be hoarded. Time itself is a mystery. And despite our desire for more time, there is no way to obtain more of it.

The parable demonstrates that one of the greatest human foibles is the idea that we own what we possess. While it is true that we can possess something, it is an illusion to believe that we can keep it. Time, like death, is the great equalizer. No matter how many things we may desire, there will never be enough time to satisfy this hunger.

One of the greatest points of hope can be found in the realization that all things are to be enjoyed, not hoarded. Some gifts are best enjoyed when given away. But to realize this truth we need time.

Not all find it. Some waste it. But the wisest among us use time to their advantage.

Letting Go
(Traditional)

A man was fleeing from a lion when suddenly he ran over the edge of a cliff. On his descent, he managed to grab hold of a small branch sticking out of the rock. Dangling over the abyss, the man began to call out for help. No one answered.

When it was obvious that he was alone, the fellow began to cry out to God, "Lord, save me!"

There was a voice from heaven, "Do you believe that I can save you? Do you trust me?"

"Yes, Lord!" the man replied.

"Good. Then let go of the branch."

• • •

Sometimes the only way out of a situation is complete surrender. When we have reached the end of all of our striving and effort, perhaps the only alternative is trust in a higher power.

The letting go is not easy, of course. We value control and self-reliance. But there is so much of life that is beyond us. Those who complete the art of surrender have learned to trust in a greater hope.

4

The Love That
Conquers All

Whoever loves is born of God, and knows God.

—1 John 4:7

There is no fear in love, for a perfected love casts out fear.

—1 John 4:18

There is an old adage: Love makes the world go 'round. Indeed, love might be described as a universal craving, the desire that nourishes us through the best and worst of life. We all have our own stories to tell with regard to love. We can recount those times and places and moments when we have experienced the love of another, or when we have held onto love as the last promise of rest and the best hope of tomorrow.

Among the world's greatest parables, there are many stories of love and forgiveness. These are parables that teach both the delights of love and the dangers of misdirected passions. These are stories that can teach us how to live more completely and more fully. And some are parables that can drive away the shadows of sorrow and loneliness.

Take, for example, this traditional Jewish tale:

Once there lived a widow who had an only son. One day this son was killed in a tragic accident. Beaten down with grief, the woman mourned her son's loss day and night, and no one was able to comfort her. Finally, a friend took the woman to a mysterious rabbi.

"I have reached the end of my rope!" the woman cried. "I beg you to plead with the Almighty that my son might be brought back to life, or that God might at least lighten my grief."

"I know a remedy for grief," the rabbi told her. "Bring me a mustard seed from a home which has never known grief. God will use this magic seed to remove the sorrow from your life."

At once the woman set out to find the magic seed. She first visited the home of a wealthy family, thinking, "Surely the rich are secure from tragedy and hardship. A family such as this has known no sorrow." After knocking on the door of the mansion, the widow explained to the woman of the house why she had come. "I am in search of a home that has known no sorrow," she said. "Is this the place? If so, I beg you to give me a mustard seed."

When the woman of the house heard this, she burst into tears. "Have I never known sorrow? Oh, you have come to the wrong house!" And she proceeded to tell the widow of all the tragedies and travails her family had endured. She even invited the widow into her home to listen to all of her heartaches, and the widow stayed on for several days, listening to all these troubles and caring for the woman of the house.

Afterwards, the widow continued her search, visiting many modest homes in the valley. But wherever she turned, the stories were much the same. Everyone, from the richest to the poorest, recounted tales of sadness and woe. And each time, the widow stayed behind in the home to listen and to care for the needs of others.

After several months, she grew so used to hearing about the sorrows of others that she forgot about her own problems and her search for the magic mustard seed, never realizing that her care for others had driven the sorrow from her life.

This parable has occupied a place in several faiths, and has been retold in a variety of forms, each with the same conclusion: love is healing.

In the telling and retelling of these parables, I trust that you will find nurture and strength. I hope these parables will compel you to love well and to lose yourself in compassion for others.

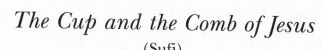

The Cup and the Comb of Jesus
(Sufi)

When Jesus walked among hills of Galilee and the streets of Judea, he carried only a cup and a comb—his only two possessions. One day, however, Jesus noticed a man drinking water from his hands. Immediately Jesus threw away his cup. Some days later, when Jesus saw a man combing his hair with his fingers, he also threw away the comb.

• • •

What is love? Is it a feeling? A decision? Or is love the ability to empathize with the plight and misfortunes of others?

Somewhere, in all of us, there is a great love waiting to break free. This is the love of service and devotion to others, our willingness to offer up a piece of ourselves. After all, the measure of our lives will not be in how much we have accumulated, but in how much we have given up.

The White Elephant and the Hunter
(Buddhist)

Queen Videha of India once dreamed of a beautiful white elephant with six ivory tusks. When she awoke, she desired these tusks more than anything else in the world. She asked the king to get them for her.

Although this was a nearly impossible task, the king loved the queen very much, and so he sent word to the finest hunters in the world that he would pay a great reward for these six ivory tusks.

Now it happened that there was indeed a beautiful white elephant with six tusks that lived in the Himalayan mountains. This elephant was training for Buddhahood and had once saved a hunter's life many years before.

But when this hunter heard of the king's reward, he was filled with greed and forgot about the elephant's past kindness toward him. The hunter packed his things and set out on a journey into the depths of the mountains in search of the great beast.

Knowing that the elephant was in training for Buddhahood, the hunter disguised himself as a monk. Approaching the elephant in the guise of a friend, the hunter walked up to the elephant and shot it with a poisoned arrow. When the other elephants saw this, they were angered, and rose up as one to kill the hunter.

But the white elephant, knowing that it was going to die, had great compassion for the hunter and forgave him for his greed. It sheltered the hunter in its giant arms and protected him from the fury of the other elephants. Then, when the danger had passed, the elephant asked the hunter why he had done such a foolish thing. The hunter broke down and confessed that he had coveted the elephant's six white tusks and the reward and praise of the king.

When the elephant heard this, it walked its last steps to a nearby tree and broke off its tusks by smashing them against the tree trunk. The elephant gave the tusks to the hunter and said, "By this offering I have now completed my training for Buddhahood and I will be reborn in the Pure Land. But when I become a Buddha, I will return to you, and will help you to rid yourself of the three poison arrows of greed, anger, and obsession."

•   •   •

This is a powerful parable of love and forgiveness, and contains the finest elements of great storytelling. The parable, while serving as a metaphor for enlightenment, can also be taken as social commentary and provides a glimpse into the destructive motives and emotions that often drive human decisions and actions. The motives of the king and queen, and especially the hunter, are laid bare in the wake of the elephant's purity and love.

There is something within the heart of humanity that quickly forgets acts of kindness and generosity. It is so easy to focus on material goods, or fame, or fortune, that one can often forget about the inner resources needed to live well. Those who have ascended to a higher spiritual plane are able to forgive those who have done wrong, or who may lack spiritual depth.

Love is the greatest power because it has the capacity to transform others. Sacrifice and relinquishment are outward signs of love.

This timeless parable demonstrates the nature of true inner peace and the self-sacrifice that leads to forgiveness and compassion—even for one's enemies.

The Men in the Mirror
(Based on a parable of Søren Kierkegaard)

Once there was a father and son who understood each other very well. When the father looked at his son he saw, as if looking into a mirror, a younger image of himself. When the son looked at his father, he imagined what he would look like in the years to come.

One day the father said to his son, "My poor child, you are going into a quiet despair." Although this was true, neither understood how to interpret the saying. Each believed he was the cause of the other's sadness.

When the father died, the son was lost for a time. But although the son felt a deep loss, he decided to focus on imitating his father. From that day on, the son comforted himself by recalling his father's words: "You are going into a quiet despair." He understood, at last, that his father loved him.

• • •

Kierkegaard (1813–1855), commonly regarded as the father of Christian existentialist philosophy, was a master storyteller who frequently used parables to illustrate his insights. In its original form, this parable attempts to demonstrate how the feelings of one person can strengthen and confirm the feelings of another. But the parable might also be helpful in revealing how love, at least in most relationships, lives in the quiet cracks and spaces of life, and how we might find strength and confidence in accepting the love of another—even when we cannot completely understand the motives and intentions of those we love.

On still another level, this story demonstrates how imitation is a by-product of love. As in most families, children grow by imitating a parent. Likewise, the parent sees himself or herself in the imitation of the child. This bond of recognition is love, and it is one of the strongest bonds we experience in life.

When this bond between parent and child is severed—either through abuse, death, or unresolved anger—there is despair. Healing comes when one is able to move beyond the loss, the words, and the feelings to find an inner peace. This may also be true of one's relationship with God, since Kierkegaard was fond of using double metaphors to describe both the physical and the spiritual world.

~

The Heart of Love
(Jewish)

There were two brothers who shared a farm. They each had their own livestock and granary, and they split the profits evenly. However, one of the brothers was married and had a large family. The other brother was single.

One day the single brother thought, "It is not fair that I receive half of the farm's profits when my brother is married and has children to care for. Why should I receive half when my brother has the greater need?"

That night he prepared a large sack of grain, carried it to the door of his brother's barn, and placed it there.

Now, the next morning, the married brother went to his barn and was startled to see that he had an extra sack of grain. He thought, "It is not fair that my brother and I divide the profits of the farm evenly. After all, I have a wife and children to care for me in my old age. My brother is alone in this world. He can use this grain more than I can."

That night, the married brother carried the sack of grain to his brother's barn and placed it at the door.

This went on for several days, with each of the brothers carrying a sack of grain to the other's barn.

One night, however, the two brothers met each other on the way, each carrying a sack of grain. They dropped the sacks, ran toward each other, and embraced, understanding at last the love they had for one another.

•   •   •

Among families, it is often difficult for love to be expressed openly. Sometimes, our actions must reveal the love we hold in our hearts. Acts of kindness, generosity of spirit, and genuinely caring for those in our own homes is the most important of all loves.

Kindness is not something we can put on in the morning, then take off at night. Kindness is an inner virtue, a way of life.

When true kindness is demonstrated in our daily actions, there is understanding and reciprocation. No kind act will ever go unnoticed. In the end, a kindness has a way of being returned in one form or another.

Inner Nature
(Buddhist)

A monk sat on the bank of a river, eager to begin his meditation. As he prepared himself, however, he noticed that a scorpion was trapped on a rock in the river. The water continued to rise, threatening to carry the scorpion away.

Moved by compassion, the monk reached down and attempted to pick up the scorpion and move it to safety. But each time he tried, the scorpion stung him on the hand.

Another monk came by and witnessed this. He said, "Don't you know that it is the scorpion's nature to sting?"

"Yes," answered the monk. "But it is my nature to save. Should I change my nature just because the scorpion does not change its nature?"

•   •   •

Compassion is most difficult when others do not return our love. As Jesus once pointed out, it is easy to love those who love us back. Loving those who might hate or injure us, however, is far more difficult, and tests the true nature of compassion. Moving into the depths of such love requires far more than meditation— it requires practice, faith, and a level of spiritual maturity.

This particular parable has been retold in other forms, but always includes a scorpion and a holy man. These extreme metaphors help to demonstrate the difficulty of loving completely. In fact, love is the most difficult work we will undertake in life. To love deeply and completely requires all the strength and stamina we possess.

But as the parable shows, the greatest love has no need to receive love in return.

❧

The Fire of Compassion
(Buddhist)

There once lived a beautiful parrot in a dense mountain thicket. This bird lived among the other animals of the forest in complete harmony and tranquility.

One day, a careless hunter started a fire, and as the wind stirred the flames the animals were swept into confusion and fear. The parrot, knowing that he could fly away to safety, was nevertheless moved by compassion for his friends.

Flying to a nearby lake, he dipped his beak into the water, flew over the flames, and shook drops of water from his beak to give relief from the heat. He did this many times with a heart burning with compassion, and did not stop until the flames were extinguished.

•   •   •

There are many instances in life where people do not know the depth of compassion found in a community until tragedy strikes. As with many disasters, we typically see communities in action when the need is greatest—after floods, fires, or hurricanes. In spite of the stresses that often tear people apart, there is something within the human spirit that longs to help others. Suffering brings out our deepest empathy.

It is also true that everyone has the capacity for this compassion. It may lie dormant until needed, but the extremes of life cause compassion to rise to the surface. There are gifts, and there are givers. And the greatest gifts are those we offer to one another through a spirit of generosity and helpfulness, expecting nothing in return.

Sometimes, it is only in tragedy that we witness the true meaning of compassion and sacrifice. But it is good to know that this is the highest calling and the better nature of humanity.

The Jewel of Creation
(Jewish)

As God was nearing the completion of creation, an announcement was made in heaven. "I wish to create a creature who will appreciate all that has been made," God said. "I will call this creature: human. These creatures will have intellect, reason, and understanding."

Then Truth came before the Almighty and said, "O God, I urge you to reconsider creating a being who is capable of lying. If you do, there will most certainly be deception and fraud let loose upon the world."

Next, Peace came near. "O God, I echo the sentiments of Truth. Let the Almighty reconsider creating a creature who is capable of upsetting the tranquillity of the earth. No doubt, if they are created, there will be revenge and war, there will be bloodshed and destruction."

Soon thereafter, Love came near, and in a soft voice said, "O God, may you not forget that any being created in your image has the capacity to perform great and noble deeds. With your Spirit, these beings will be able to shelter one another, care for the sick and lonely, and will no doubt bring glory to you in their capacity to love deeply."

And so it was that, although God heard the voices of Truth and Peace, it was the voice of Love that prevailed in the creation of humanity.

• • •

There are moments when every person is aware of the human bent toward violence and destruction. One need only read the daily newspaper or watch the evening news to see examples.

But there are moments equal to, if not greater than these truths, when we glimpse the amazing quality of love among people—acts of selflessness, acts of heroism and sacrifice. These are the better angels of our nature.

This unique parable places God at the center of love's persuasion, making all things possible, including the creation of the world. The story reminds us that not even the Creator is exempt from seeing the power of love and that love is, first and foremost, a reason to continue with any endeavor.

Truth may change minds; peace may change the world; but only love has the power to change the human heart, making truth and peace possible.

Portraits of the World
(Based on a parable of Søren Kierkegaard)

There were two artists. One said, "I have traveled the world, but have been unable to find a man worth painting. Whenever I see a face, I note only the flaws and deficiencies. Therefore I seek in vain."

The other said, "I have not traveled the world. My work has kept me close to home. But when I look at the faces of those closest to me, I see that each one's flaws and deficiencies mask at least one redeeming quality. Therefore I paint, and am satisfied."

• • •

Are people worth loving? Surely, if we look closely enough, we can see the best qualities in one another.

Many of Kierkegaard's parables point to these deeper truths and call us to love and recognize the value of others. Reminiscent of many of the apocryphal stories about DaVinci, this wonderful story blends vocation and observation to offer an insight on the human condition.

People are flawed. We have cracks in our armor, skeletons in our closets. However, those who take the time to see beyond the flaws in others reap a great reward.

There is a beauty in life that often goes unrecognized. But when we discover the worth of those around us, we begin to live more fully.

The Three Rings
(Jewish)

There was a father who had three sons and a magic ring. This magic ring had the power to bestow the gifts of kindness, generosity, and grace to the one who possessed it, and the father had used it well his entire life.

Eventually, however, the time came when the father knew he was dying. Unwilling to give the magic ring to only one of his sons, he sent the ring to a jeweler and asked that two other identical rings be made. Afterwards, he called his sons together and told them, "I have loved you my entire life, and now I must pass along to you my most cherished possession. I give each of you a magic ring. These rings will bestow kindness, generosity, and grace. Use the rings well, that you may have a long life and prosper with God's help."

Now, after the father died, the sons believed that only one of them actually had the magic ring. They began to argue and complain. Each believed that another brother had the magic ring. Eventually they took the rings to a judge and demanded, "Tell us which of these is the magic ring!"

The judge answered, "It is impossible to tell by looking at the rings. I would suggest we wait, and watch to see who lives the most virtuous life—like your father. The one who lives well will be the one who, obviously, possesses the magic ring."

Each of the brothers agreed to this idea. And each of the brothers lived as if he possessed the magic ring. From that day forward, each of the brothers was filled with goodness, thoughtfulness, and honesty.

•   •   •

The virtues of goodness and love are not derived from props or magic. Love comes from the heart, and is demonstrated by the way we live. There are no shortcuts.

It is possible, however, to pass along signs and symbols that may remind others of these virtues, and assist others in the striving toward a better life. Nearly all faiths have relics and rituals that are aimed at pointing others toward a more virtuous existence.

The real magic, of course, occurs when we live a virtuous life simply because we want to, with no aim but to please others, and no thought of gain. The greatest proof of a life well lived is not the possessions we hold in the hand, but the attributes we hold in the heart.

A Vision of Heaven and Hell
(Jewish)

A righteous man was allowed to see heaven and hell. First he was ushered to hell, where he saw people seated at a most alluring banquet table. The people seated at the table appeared emaciated and frail, as if they had not eaten in weeks. Near each of them, however, were heaping plates of food.

"Why don't the people partake of the food?" the man asked his guide.

"Ah, well," said the guide, "as you can see, each person at the table has arms that cannot bend. They are unable to feed themselves."

"Truly this is hell," said the man.

Later, the man was ushered to heaven, where he beheld much the same scene: a large festive table laden with food, and people whose arms could not bend. These people, however, were not starving and weak, but happy and well fed.

"I don't understand," said the man. "Heaven appears to be no different than hell."

"Yes," said the guide, "but with one noticeable exception. Here the people are happy and well fed. In hell they think only of feeding themselves. In heaven they have learned to feed each other."

•   •   •

In a world of plenty and starvation, it is no wonder that some images of heaven and hell center on food. Love is far more than a feeling. Love compels our hands, moves our hearts toward each other. Love is a verb. The love that can change the world is a movement of the spirit.

Muhammad and the Cat
(Islamic)

Muhammad was teaching in the desert, reciting from the Koran to a group of spellbound listeners. As he was speaking, a sick cat meandered into the camp, sidled up to Muhammad, and went to sleep on the hem of his exquisite robe.

Now Muhammad was unaware of this cat, even though he continued to speak for the remainder of the day. All day the cat slept on the hem of his robe, finding warmth and healing in the shadow of the prophet.

When the day came to an end, everyone returned to their tents for the evening. But the prophet, seeing the cat asleep on his robe, took a sharp knife and cut off the hem of his robe where the cat was sleeping. In this way the prophet destroyed the most beautiful of garments, but left the cat undisturbed in its slumber.

• • •

Does love have boundaries? Perhaps not. There may be moments in life when we are called upon to extend love in ways we never imagined. Sometimes sacrifices are required. Sometimes we must trade one priority for another. A heartfelt compassion can move a person to strange acts of kindness. Love, after all, is the greatest power in the world.

5

The Power of Friendship

*A good story in Judaism is not about miracles, but about
friendship and hope—the greatest miracles of all.*

—Elie Wiesel

In Christian tradition, there is a parable attributed to the
Desert Fathers that goes like this:

A brother came to Father Matoes and asked, "What shall I do?
Whenever I am among people, I cannot seem to control my
tongue. I speak out of turn, I condemn people for their good
deeds, and I contradict them constantly. What am I to do?"

The old man gave this answer: "If you cannot control yourself, you need to get away from people. Go live alone. Those
who live among people must be round, not square. They must
be able to turn toward others."

"But you live alone," the brother pointed out.

"Ah, yes," said the old man. "But I live alone not because
of my virtue, but because of my weakness. Those who live
among people are the strong ones."

In a rapidly changing world, it is not always easy to maintain friendships or to nurture relationships. Many people live in
constant transition—a new opportunity here, a new job there,
pulling up stakes one day, trying to put down roots the next.

One fact remains, however. There is a human need for contact
with others. Friendship—or socializing with others—is essential

for a healthy society. Lasting friendships are built on trust and support.

However, it takes patience and effort to nurture friendships in a fast-paced world. To live among people and to embrace friends in a hectic world truly requires strength.

Common to many parables, the themes of friendship, trust, and mutual respect can be demonstrated time and again. Here we find some of the best and brightest gems that can help us to rekindle the flame of friendship, reminding us that we do not walk through life alone.

The Eagle's Eggs
(African)

Once there was a beautiful mother eagle that soared over the earth. It had the power to heal and the power to bless.

One day, while it was soaring on the winds, the eagle noticed an old woman who was having trouble walking. The eagle swooped down to help and asked the old woman, "What kind of sore is that on your leg?"

The old woman answered, "I have had it for many years, but I have grown too old to do anything about it."

The eagle said, "I would do something good for you, but experience tells me that people do not remember their friends."

"Oh, not me!" insisted the old woman. "I would never forget my friends. And I would never forget a good deed."

So the eagle said, "In that case, I will heal you. Close your eyes."

The woman did as she was instructed, and when she opened her eyes, the sore on her leg was gone.

"Close your eyes again," the eagle said.

The woman closed her eyes, and when she opened them, the forest had been cleared.

"Close your eyes a third time," said the eagle.

When the woman opened her eyes, she saw a serene little village, with houses, streets, and a marketplace.

"All of this is yours," the eagle said. "All I ask is that you remember that I am your friend. If you do not forget this one thing, you will be blessed."

"Oh, I will never forget," the old woman said. "I would give you anything you ask. You are a friend for life."

"Good," said the eagle. "Now I have but one favor to ask. All I ask is that I might build my nest and raise my children in the silk-cotton tree that stands at the center of the village."

"Of course," the old woman agreed. "It is yours." And with that word, she hurried off to live in the village. The eagle lighted in the silk-cotton tree and laid her eggs.

Now it came to pass that the old woman's grandchildren came to live with her. Every day these children stood at the center of the village and admired the eagle nesting on her eggs. Soon, however, they began to wonder how large the eggs were, and what they might taste like for breakfast.

"Give us the eagle's eggs," the grandchildren demanded one day. But the old woman remembered what the eagle had done for her, so she adamantly refused.

Each day, however, the grandchildren grew louder and more demanding in their whining. "Give us the eagle's eggs for breakfast!" they shouted. "Give us the eagle's eggs." This went on for some time until the old woman thought she would be driven mad with the complaints and demands of her grandchildren.

Finally, wanting some peace and quiet in her home, the old woman told the grandchildren in a moment of weakness, "Cut down the silk-cotton tree and bring me the eggs!"

That morning the children and all of the other villagers gathered around the tree in the center of town and began to saw it down. The mother eagle was not in her nest, and when the tree came crashing down, she did not see it.

Minutes later, the old woman cooked the eagle's eggs for her grandchildren.

Now, when the mother eagle returned, she was startled to find her tree missing, and the nest along with it. "Where are my children?" she cried. "Where are they?"

One of the villagers told the eagle, "The old woman has cooked the eggs for her grandchildren to eat."

The eagle flew to the old woman's house and said, "Have you forgotten so soon the first law of friendship?" Then the eagle flapped her wings, and the village and the people disappeared. She flapped her beautiful wings a second time, and all of the houses crumbled away, and the forest reappeared. She flapped her wings a third time, and the old woman's sore returned to her leg.

Then the eagle said, "Now your eyes at last are opened. I was your friend, but you returned evil for good."

●　　●　　●

What is the first law of friendship? As this parable demonstrates, it is the virtue of faithfulness. Those who take without giving, or who forget a friend in need, will not have friends for long. The first lesson of friendship is that when we learn to give, we will also receive.

Many African parables, such as this one, commonly incorporate nature into the story as well as aspects of community and village life. The parables were used not only to teach a lesson, but also to strengthen village life and dedication.

This story also implies that we should honor our promises, regardless of changing circumstances.

Two Friends and a Bear
(Aesop)

Two friends were hiking through the woods when a bear suddenly appeared. One ran away, leaving his friend behind, and climbed into a tree for safety. The other friend, realizing he had been left alone, fell to the ground and acted as if he were dead.

The bear approached, sniffed at the man, and, believing him to be a corpse, went on its way.

Later, the man who had hidden in the tree came down and asked his friend, "What did the bear whisper in your ear?"

The other answered, "In the future, do not travel with friends who run away when there is danger."

●   ●   ●

A friend may be defined as one who is present during times of trouble. Those who run away from responsibility, or walk away from a friend in need, are rarely remembered for their courage. As William Howard Taft once said, "Too many people do not care what happens as long as it does not happen to them."

This story by Aesop reminds us that it is always wise to think of others first, especially when danger is present. By saving another from harm, we may also be saving ourselves.

An Image of Peacefulness
(Desert Fathers)

Some old men came to see Father Poemen. "Sometimes," they said, "we see a friend sleeping during the worship of God. What should we do—pinch him to keep him awake?"

"Actually," Father Poemen said, "if I saw a friend sleeping, I would put his head on my knees and let him sleep."

●   ●   ●

Sometimes the smallest acts meet the greatest needs. Kindness is not necessarily found in grand display or daring deeds, but in the daily spaces of life.

A friend is one who knows what another needs, and offers a remedy that is both helpful and unassuming. Sometimes the real test comes when others challenge a friendship. Imagination and compromise are sometimes needed to keep a friendship strong.

Friendship Is Its Own Reward
(Jewish)

There was a country that valued hospitality and fine horses above all things. A farmer lived there who had the most beautiful horse in all the land. Everyone wanted this horse, and not a day went by that someone did not stop at the man's farm and make an offer for the animal. Unable to part with the horse, however, the farmer always refused the offers.

But as time passed, the farmer eventually fell on hard times. Others recognized that the farmer was not doing well, and one day the farmer's best friend decided that this would be a good time to bid on the horse. "After all," the friend thought, "I can pay a high price for the horse and my friend's finances will be restored."

According to custom, they made a date to sit down to dinner and discuss the matter before transacting business. The friend arrived, sat down to dinner, and the two men ate their fill of delicious meat.

After supper, the friend said, "I would like to make an offer on your horse. I will be generous, since I know you need the money."

But the farmer replied, "The horse is no longer for sale. When I heard that you were coming to dinner, I had nothing to serve. I did not want to be inhospitable. So I killed the animal and offered him up as the main course."

•   •   •

In friendship, sacrifices must often be made. Some of these sacrifices may be extreme. But the reward is great.

According to this parable, hospitality is more important than proper decorum or business. Even when life is tough, it is important to practice hospitality. In fact, a gift offered during a tough time will be all the more valued by the recipient. A sacrifice demonstrates depth of character and shows how much we care.

A Day and Night
(Jewish)

A rabbi sat near the campfire with a group of students. He asked the question, "How can we know when the night has ended and the day has begun?"

Looking up at the stars, one of the students offered an answer. "You know the night is over and the day has begun when you can look into the distance and deduce which animal is your dog and which is your sheep."

The rabbi replied, "This is a good answer, but it is not the answer I am looking for."

Another student spoke. "You know the night is over and the day has begun when sunlight falls upon the leaves and you can tell the difference between a palm tree and a fig tree."

"Again a good answer," the rabbi said. "But it is not the answer I am looking for."

Unable to think of other answers to the riddle, the students finally said, "Tell us, Rabbi. Answer your own question. How can one tell when the night is over and the day has begun?"

The rabbi answered, "When you can look into the eyes of a human being and see a friend, you know that it is morning. If you cannot see a friend, you know it is still night."

•　　•　　•

Friendship begins when a person recognizes the value of another— not for the sake of personal gain, but for the reward of knowing that person for his or her own sake. When we make a friend our lives are strengthened. When we reject another person as a friend, usually our lives are diminished.

In Jewish parables especially, riddles are often used to engage the reader or listener in seeking a solution to the puzzle. Originally, the oral form of this story may have contained a pause for the purpose of allowing the audience to offer their own solutions to the riddle. Some of these answers, no doubt, might have been incorporated into the next telling. In this way, the parable would continue to gather power and credibility, as new and better solutions were offered in each retelling.

By using the common images of day and night, light and darkness, the parable also lends itself to symbolism and memory, and may have been told at those times of the day when people were gathered together for laughter or special occasions.

The Ant and the Pigeon
(Aesop)

An ant went to the stream to get a drink but got caught in the current and was about to be swept away. Seeing this, a pigeon on a nearby limb broke off a twig and tossed it into the stream, saving the ant's life.

Moments later, a hunter appeared with a trap, readying to catch the pigeon. Seeing this, the ant bit the hunter's foot, causing him to drop the trap, and the pigeon flew away.

•   •   •

As with many of Aesop's parables, there are common sayings that one can often attach to them. Here, the old adage still applies: One good turn deserves another.

Friendly Advice
(Buddhist)

There once lived a man who was easily angered. Small misunderstandings, petty concerns, and even well-intended remarks would often send him into a rage.

One day, two of his friends were talking in front of the house where this man lived. Both of them began to remark on his terrible temper. "Deep down, he is a nice person," one said, "until he becomes impatient or agitated."

"Yes," said the other, "he has the seeds of kindness, and yet small things can cause his emotions to boil over."

The man, overhearing what the friends were saying about him, fell into a rage. He ran after these friends and drove them away.

•   •   •

A friend's opinion is a valuable thing, and only a true friend is able to offer constructive criticism. Although criticism is difficult for us to accept, when offered in a spirit of caring, it has the potential to make us better. On the other hand, ignoring a friend's opinion can cause a rift in the relationship. Those who can't accept friendly advice make poor neighbors.

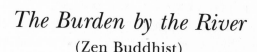

The Burden by the River
(Zen Buddhist)

Two monks were walking along the bank of a swift river. There they met a young woman who could not cross alone. One of the monks picked up the young woman and carried her across the river to the other side.

Some time later, the other monk said to his companion, "Did you forget that it is against the rules to touch a woman? Have you forgotten the vows you have taken?"

The other monk answered, "Brother, I left the young woman on the bank of the river. Are you still carrying her?"

• • •

Rules, self-imposed restrictions, and social taboos can often get in the way of friendship. Some barriers can keep people from helping each other or offering assistance to someone in need. In every society there are unspoken rules that suppress interaction between people. A friend, however, is one who does not call attention to the rules that have been broken, but to the charity that has been extended.

This parable reminds us that there are greater measures of friendship than rules and laws. Vows are fine, as far as they go, but in the end the very nature of humanity calls one person to help another in a time of need. Some needs must be met. And there lies within each person the ability to meet a need.

Forgetting a wrong done, or an inflicted hurt, is a step toward freedom. When we continue to bring up past wrongs, we betray an inability to forgive. True freedom, as well as true friendship, is being able to leave the past behind in order to embrace the future.

A Stone's Throw
(Jewish)

A man became angry with his friend. Noticing a large stone on the ground, he swore an oath that he would hurl it at his friend. But, moments later, the man changed his mind and repented of his anger. He thought, "I have sworn an oath that I would throw the stone. Yet, if I do, my friend will be killed. Still, I must keep the oath."

With that thought, the man picked up the stone, broke it into small pebbles, and threw these at his friend one by one. In such a manner the man kept his oath, and also spared the life of a friend.

•   •   •

However this parable may be interpreted—as the wisdom to flee from anger, or the importance of keeping oaths—the end points to the importance of being patient and gentle to one's friends. In friendship, as in life, one often is faced with several choices—not all of which offer an acceptable outcome. But by choosing the best path, one can display wisdom. Sometimes the best alternative is to decide between the lesser of two evils.

On another level, the parable also demonstrates that it is better to offer small doses of criticism or a few thoughts at appropriate times, than it is to hurl massive insults that could kill a friendship. Small mistakes and misunderstandings can be forgiven far more easily than assaults on another's character or integrity.

When faced with a difficult choice, the parable reminds us to choose wisely or to wait for a solution that might be revealed at a later time.

The Greatest Treasure
(Jewish)

There was a father who pledged to give each of his ten children an inheritance of one hundred golden coins. He was wealthy when he made the promise, but as he neared the end of life, money was in short supply. Eventually it became apparent he would be unable to fulfill his promise.

Hours before his death, the father called his children to his bedside. He began to give each of the children the money he had pledged. To each of the first nine, he was able to fulfill his word, giving them one hundred gold coins. But when it was time to pay his youngest daughter, he requested that the other children leave the room.

"My daughter," the father said, "I am unable to give you one hundred gold coins. Here, you may have twenty coins, for it is all that remains."

At once the daughter protested, "But Father, if you knew you would be unable to give me one hundred coins, why didn't you adjust the amounts you gave to the other nine?"

"Better that I should fulfill my word to as many of my children as possible," the father said. "However, I have something of far greater value than gold which I give in place of the coins. I offer you my ten best friends. Their love and support has been worth more to me than all the gold in the world. As a final request, I would ask that you treat these friends well." And with that word, the father died.

Now it happened that the nine older children immediately took a liking to their wealth. Some bought houses, some land. Others left on extended vacations.

The youngest daughter stayed at home with her twenty gold coins and grew more and more despondent. One day, however, she remembered her father's final request, and decided to invite her father's friends to an extravagant dinner. She spent her entire inheritance on the invitations, the dinner, and on bottles of fine wine.

When her father's friends arrived, she gave each of them a seat of honor, provided entertainment, and made certain that each had his fill of good food. After the dinner the ten friends said to one another, "Of all the children, the youngest daughter is the only one who has displayed the integrity of her father. Let us return the kindness."

And so it was that each of the ten friends gave the daughter one hundred gold coins, thus fulfilling the saying, "Friendship is more valuable than gold."

• • •

Perhaps this parable needs no explanation, but it is worth noting that there are two lessons to be found in this story.

First, we see the importance of integrity and keeping our promises. In the father's gifts, we understand the importance of honoring our word. The fact that the father kept his word to nine, rather than none, has significance. In doing so, he honored his promise rather than compromise it.

The other lesson, of course, is to be found in the value of friendship. There is no measure for the worth of a friend, and there are times when a friend will provide more assistance than a bank account.

The story reminds us of the proverb:

Make new friends, but keep the old;
One is silver, the other gold.

The Difference between a Ditch
and a Mound
(Jewish)

There were two farmers whose fields were very near to one another. One farmer, however, had a ditch in the middle of his field. The other had a mound in the center.

The man who owned the mound wondered, "When will I get a ditch?"

And the man who owned the ditch wondered, "When will I get a mound?"

One day the two farmers met along the road and the owner of the ditch said, "Sell me your mound."

The other replied, "O, how I wish you had made such a request long ago. You may have it for nothing!"

• • •

Profit is not the primary goal in life. Sometimes convenience is a greater prize. A friend is one who meets another's need with warmth and generosity. And when offered, such gifts of the spirit are usually reciprocated.

This parable demonstrates how needs can be met through mutual sacrifice. Because people do not prize the same things, friendships can often be enriched through simple acts of generosity and awareness of a friend's need.

It is still the case: One man's meat is another man's poison.

❧

Many Roots
(Jewish)

A reed grew alongside a river. As time went by, it continued to produce young shoots. Because its roots were many, when the winds came, it was not uprooted from its place. It blew from side to side, but when the winds subsided, it stood up straight and firm again.

The cedar, on the other hand, did not grow along the river. It did not produce new shoots, and its roots were few. When the winds came and blew upon it, it was quickly uprooted and tossed from its place.

•   •   •

This Talmudic parable is not specifically about friendship, but it points to the relationship between depth of character, strength, integrity, and survival. The person with many friends is like one with many roots, while the person who attempts to stand alone in this world will more likely be tossed and turned by life's inevitable stresses.

Friendships deepen our ability to cope with the storms of life. And since storms come to all, it is important to rely on the power of friendship to see us through.

❧

Bearing the Burden
(Buddhist)

A wise man and his disciples took up residence in a town. Soon thereafter, a wicked man began to circulate false stories about them. This made it very difficult for the wise man and his disciples to earn a living or to teach, as others soon joined the fray and began to heap on abuse after abuse.

One of the disciples said, "It would be better for us to move to another town. There must be friendlier communities elsewhere."

The wise teacher answered, "But suppose the next town is like this? Where will we go then?"

"To yet another," was the reply.

"But there is no end to this," the wise teacher answered. "It is far better that we remain here and bear the abuse patiently until it ceases. In life there is slander and honor, praise and abuse, suffering and pleasure. But the enlightened are not controlled by external circumstances. Such abuses and delights will cease as quickly as they come."

•   •   •

Another insight about enlightenment, this parable is a reminder that friends stand together through times of difficulty and bear burdens with patience and wisdom. Tough times never last. But tough people do. Those who understand this truth have found a security within themselves and are not easily discouraged by defeat, criticism, or obstacles.

It is good to remember that pain is as fleeting as pleasure— pain just seems to last longer and is more pronounced because it is more difficult to bear. But a friend is one who can help us through difficult times by either bearing some of the burden, or reminding us of the joys and blessings we have received.

The Patience of a Friend
(Jewish)

One day the patriarch Abraham saw a man walking through the desert. He invited the traveler into his tent to dine and spend the night. Of course, the fellow eagerly accepted the hospitality.

However, as Abraham was preparing the meal, he learned that his guest was a pagan. Abraham asked the man to leave without giving him so much as a fig to eat.

That night God appeared to Abraham in a dream and asked, "Why did you treat your guest so poorly?"

Abraham replied, "Because he did not worship you, the one true God."

God said, "But Abraham, I have put up with that unbeliever for eighty years. Couldn't you have endured him for one night?"

•　　•　　•

Perhaps the true test of friendship has nothing to do with enjoying the company of people we like, but with enduring the people we can scarcely tolerate. A cornerstone of friendship is hospitality. Welcoming the stranger, particularly, is one of life's greatest challenges. Learning to smile at a stranger is one way to demonstrate friendship, but learning to appreciate those who disagree with us is far more rewarding.

When we turn someone away, we miss an opportunity to expand our world.

6

❧

Embracing the Freedom to Live

Those of calm and happy natures will hardly feel the pressure of age.

—Plato

The desire for freedom is one of the strongest motivators in life. It is a gift we often take for granted, but also one of the most difficult gifts to obtain. This is true not only on a larger social scale, but is also true on a personal level. We desire the freedom to pursue our own interests and goals, the freedom to achieve our dreams. Freedom, in all its varieties, is also a component in many remarkable stories.

A citizen might speak of personal freedom, a writer of freedom of the press. An ascetic might regard freedom as the release from the physical trappings of the world, while the devout might speak of freedom of religion. There are individual freedoms and communal ones, freedoms of the mind and freedoms of the spirit. For an expectant mother, birth is freedom, and for the gravely ill, death comes as relief.

Likewise, freedom encompasses the intangible and the mysterious. Some may have freedom, yet still be bound; others might live in chains, yet sing joyous songs. Freedom is elusive; that is why we crave it as much as love or companionship.

The parables in this chapter offer many expressions of freedom. Through these windows, we might find some wisdom for living out our days, a gentle release, or perhaps the key to a richer life. Some tell of a journey, others a destination. But in the end, the stories themselves offer us glimpses of freedom—of the body, mind, and spirit.

True Enlightenment
(Zen Buddhist)

The master Gutei used to raise his finger whenever he was asked a question about Zen. A young disciple would often imitate him in this way. Whenever someone asked, "What did the master talk about today?" the young disciple would raise his finger.

Gutei heard about this mischief, and after seizing the boy, he cut off his finger. The disciple cried and ran away, but Gutei called out to him. When the disciple turned around, Gutei raised his finger. In that moment the disciple was enlightened.

•　　•　　•

To be enlightened, in Zen Buddhism, is to transcend the pain and negativity of this world. Freedom from desire enables one to transcend and conquer. The parable demonstrates this enlightenment and the opposing forces of pain and pleasure, good and evil, which are so much a part of Zen philosophy.

The parable may also show that pain is a necessary part of learning. Without pain, there can be no growth.

Freedom often accompanies the realization that we have lost something and in its place gained something greater. Not all knowledge is helpful. And sometimes the greatest achievements are obtained only after we have given up the things that were holding us back.

Matters of the Heart
(Jewish)

A famous rabbi posed this question to his disciples: "What should a person strive for most in life?"

"To have a good eye," answered Rabbi Yacov.

"To be a good friend," answered Rabbi Yeshua.

"To be a good neighbor," answered Rabbi Yose.

"To obtain wisdom," answered Rabbi Simeon.

"To have a good heart," answered Rabbi Eliezer.

The famous rabbi nodded and said, "The words of Eliezer are most profound, as his answer includes all of the others."

Later, the famous rabbi posed another question: "What should a person avoid most in life?"

"An evil eye," answered Rabbi Yacov.

"An evil friend," answered Rabbi Yeshua.

"An evil neighbor," answered Rabbi Yose.

"One who borrows but doesn't return," said Rabbi Simeon.

"A bad heart," answered Rabbi Eliezer.

Again the rabbi said, "Eliezer's answer is most pleasing, as his includes all the others."

•   •   •

There is a saying: "No one is truly free who does not possess a pure heart." Or, as Jesus once taught, "From the heart comes all manner of evil."

This simple teaching reminds us that life is far more a matter of the heart than of the mind. What we choose to do with our time, our energy, our resources, and our talents is often dictated by our values and priorities. Those who strive for goodness within, and surround themselves with goodness, will reap many rewards.

The Poor Artist
(Buddhist)

A poor artist left his home and his wife to seek his fortune. After three years of struggle, he had saved three hundred pieces of gold and decided to return home.

On his journey back, however, he happened to pass by a grand temple in which a delightful ceremony was taking place. The artist was so impressed by the pomp and splendor of the temple that he thought to himself: "All this time I have been thinking only of myself and my fortune. But I have not considered true happiness. I must plant seeds of joy if I am to obtain what is truly worthy." And so he gave all of his worldly goods to the temple.

When the artist returned home, his wife was much dismayed by his lack of support and the fact that he had nothing to show for his three years of labor. He replied that he had invested his money. When his wife pressed him to reveal where he had placed the money, the artist told her he had given it to the monks at a certain temple.

Enraged by this behavior, the wife scolded her husband and took the matter before the local judge. When the judge asked the husband for his defense, he said that he had not acted foolishly but had invested the money for future happiness by planting seeds of good fortune. He said, "When I came to the temple, it seemed like a good place to plant seed, much like a farmer plants in a fertile field. When I gave the monks the gold, I felt all worldly desire and greed melt away, and I experienced true freedom. Wealth, you see, is not found in gold, but in the mind."

The judge was impressed with the artist's answer and so dismissed the case. Those in the courtroom who heard of this verdict were equally impressed and from that day on began to help the artist in various ways. In this manner, the artist and his wife entered into a better state of good fortune than at first, and they lived together happily all their days.

• • •

This story demonstrates that when we hoard possessions, we may actually lose them—a common theme in many cultures. This traditional Buddhist parable reveals a relationship between friendship and fortune: by giving to others, we are enriched in ways that cannot be measured in material terms.

The story is faintly reminiscent of Jesus's teaching about material possessions and the need to give away the things that might prevent us from experiencing true grace and freedom.

When we focus on possessions, we worry about losing them rather than seeing what we may gain through sharing. Those who focus on relationships have the potential to experience more joy.

As the saying goes: Some live to work; others work to live. The differences are astounding.

Opening Doors
(Zen Buddhist)

A father arrived home to find that his house had been set ablaze. Not far from the house, he noticed a small corpse, which he presumed to be his son, smoldering in the embers. The father burned the corpse and committed the ashes to the ground.

Some months later, however, the son returned home— for some thieves had actually kidnapped the child. The boy knocked on the door at midnight, waking his father. "Let me in!" the boy shouted.

"Who is it?" the father wanted to know.

"Your son!"

"You cannot be my son," the father said. "He is dead, and I have already buried him."

And so the father refused to let his son into the house and lost him a second time.

• • •

What is this parable about? Missed opportunities, perhaps? The human inability to accept the miraculous? Or maybe it is a story about life itself—the cruel, heartless, twists of fate that often separate families, friends, lovers.

Regardless of what we might see in this story, there is an element of sadness here that points us in a healing direction: there is always the possibility of regaining what we have lost. Life is about opening doors, letting others in, welcoming and accepting what we might otherwise shut out in our ignorance or self-centeredness.

What have you lost? How are you trying to regain it?

The Bracelets of Buddhahood
(Buddhist)

There was a king of Benares who lived in splendor and pleasure. On hot days, he would recline on his couch, which was adorned with precious stones and gold. A female servant would massage him with fragrant ointment.

This servant wore a great many bracelets on her arm, and as she massaged the king, the bracelets would jangle together, making a sound that irritated the king. He asked the servant to remove the bracelets.

The servant began to do this. She removed one bracelet, then a second. There was less sound. She continued to remove bracelets until there were only two—these made very little sound. At last she removed the final bracelet, and there was no sound but pure pleasure.

At that moment the king had an awakening. "This is what I should do with my kingdom," he said. "I will strip myself of my ministers, my servants, my subjects, my concubines, and my waiting attendants. I will rid myself of all excesses, all bothersome transactions and business of the kingdom."

From that moment on the king had no worldly desires, but spent his time meditating in pure silence until he became a Buddha.

•　　•　　•

The greatest obstacles to freedom may often be found in our attachment to excesses and accumulation—the desire for things. As the previous two parables attest, one can obtain freedom by stripping away all that is not essential, all that is excess. What remains is happiness and peace, the greatest freedoms of all.

A Life of Leisure
(Jewish)

A young donkey complained to his father one evening after a hard day's work. "There is no justice in this life," the donkey said. "You and I slave away on this farm every day, pulling heavy loads and plowing fields. Yet the pig makes his leisure in the sun, getting fatter with each passing day. We scarcely get enough to cover our ribs, yet the pig has his fill of the slop."

"Never judge by appearance," the older donkey said. "We are the ones with the true blessing and the freedom. The pig's leisure will one day be his end. When he gets a bit fatter, the master will kill him."

●   ●   ●

This unique parable (featuring a Jewish pig, no less) points out the relationship between work and freedom. Those who enjoy the greatest freedoms are often those who make the most of their opportunities. A life free of stress and meaning ultimately produces little blessing. The freedoms we appreciate most are those we achieve through labor and sacrifice.

A life of simple leisure may seem desirable, but in the end there is little to show for it. A life is what one makes from day-to-day living, the work one produces, and the people one influences.

To have work to do is far greater than to have no work at all. Everyone needs a purpose in life.

❧

The Mystery of the Palm Wine
(African)

A tribal chief invited all the men of his village to participate in a festival. "Food is provided," he said, "but each man must bring one jug of palm wine."

Now in the village there lived a common man who had no palm wine. He thought to himself, "There is a way to go to the festival without expense. I will find an empty jug, fill the jug with water, and add it to the great pot of palm wine. My bit of water in the mix will not be noticed, and everyone will believe that I brought wine."

In this manner the man went to the festival and added his water to the mix.

During the festival, the time came for the chief to speak. He instructed the servants to fill each man's glass with palm wine. But when the guests raised their glasses, they were surprised to find that they were drinking water. Each of the guests had brought a jug of water, believing that his little bit would not spoil the pot of wine.

• • •

We may be free to act according to our desires, but not all choices, however free, lead to good ends. It is always best to follow our ethics and beliefs.

Likewise, true freedom is not license to do anything we desire. Our concern for family, the community, and for the greatest good must take precedence over individual choices. The best decisions are those that honor others and bring dignity to our reputation.

The Lesson of the Nerreh Tree
(African)

There were three brothers who had set out on a journey to another village in order to find themselves brides. On the way they saw a nerreh tree that was beginning to bear fruit. This being one of their favorite fruits, they stopped to get a better look. When they observed that the fruit was not quite ripe, they decided they would stop on their way back to pick the fruit and would share it among themselves.

Some days later, after each of the brothers had found a suitable bride, they were on their way home when they stopped to celebrate at the nerreh tree. The first brother climbed the tree and began to gather fruit. But after some time of tossing the fruit down to his brothers, he grew worried that the other two might eat all the fruit while he was busy picking. Because he wanted to keep a close eye on his brothers, he bent too far over in the tree, fell down, and died.

Now the other two brothers needed a sack to carry the fruit on their journey home. One of the brothers went to look for a sack, but he too was so worried about the other brother eating the fruit, that he began walking backwards in order to keep an eye on him. Suddenly he came upon a well, fell into it, and drowned.

The remaining brother was so pleased to have all the fruit that he sat down, at last, to eat. But just as he was about to take the first bite, a fly began buzzing around his face and would not go away. The brother started chasing the fly to kill it, tripped over a rock, and died.

Which of the three was the greediest?

•   •   •

In African tradition it is customary for the groom and his family to meet the bride's family prior to the wedding. Using this backdrop as the setting for the story, this humorous parable offers a somewhat different set of lenses through which we might glimpse the aftermath of greed. Greed is desire turned inward, and when greed is out of control, we cannot see life clearly.

In its own way, this zany tale points out the dangers of unbridled desire.

The Coconut Trap
(Hindu)

A hunter went out to catch a monkey. Taking half a coconut, he hollowed it out and drilled a hole in one end. Then, placing the coconut atop a tempting bit of food, the hunter fastened the coconut to the ground.

When a monkey came by, it reached its hand into the coconut to grab the food beneath, but was unable to pull its hand back through the coconut with a closed fist.

In this way the hunter caught many monkeys. Each monkey thought it was imprisoned. None opened its hand in order to obtain its freedom.

•   •   •

Human hands can take many forms. An open hand can signify generosity and friendship. An upturned palm can be a sign of submission. A closed fist can signify anger or greed. An unclenched fist can signify release.

One who has learned to release anger, greed, and selfishness has found freedom. When we learn to give up what is insignificant, to let go of the past, to release what is trifling, we gain a new measure of freedom.

Metamorphosis
(Taoist)

Chang Chou once dreamed he was a beautiful butterfly. In his dream he was happy, darting to and fro and flying wherever he wished. The dream was so real that he forgot that he was Chou. Suddenly he awoke to find that, indeed, he was Chou. But he was uncertain if Chou had dreamed he was a butterfly, or if a butterfly had dreamed that he was Chou.

• • •

Who has not experienced a moment of pure joy or a moment filled with awesome beauty and clarity? This is the dreamlike quality being addressed in this parable.

Sometimes we experience these moments in solitude. Sometimes they come to us as we stand admiring a beautiful sunset or an awesome mountain peak. Or they may be found in special, fleeting moments, such as during a wedding, a funeral, or in quiet conversation.

In some cultures, as this Taoist parable demonstrates, the lines between waking and dreaming are often blurred. And how often have we all said (in a moment of joy), "Pinch me so I'll know this is not a dream"?

The Magic Purse
(Jewish)

Once there was a poor man who thought of nothing but riches. As fate would have it, one day he found a small purse lying on the floor of his house. When he opened the purse, a voice declared, "Inside you will find a single coin. When you remove it, another will appear in its place. Take as many as you wish, but you may not spend a single coin until you throw the purse in the river, where it will turn into a fish."

Sure enough, when the man opened the purse, he found a single coin. When he removed it, another appeared in its place. For the remainder of the day, the man pulled coins from the purse until he had filled a large sack.

The next morning, the fellow was famished. However, he could not bear the thought of parting with any of his coins, so he went out onto the street to beg. After someone gave him a few cents, he bought bread. That evening, he drew another sack of coins from the magic purse.

The following day, he was famished again, but he could not bring himself to throw the purse into the river so he could spend his fortune. He kept the purse, and returned to the streets to beg.

This was the case day after day. The man would go to the river with the intent to throw away the purse, but would end up begging on the street. Years later, after the man died, they discovered a house full of coins. However, there was not a single crust of bread to be found anywhere in the home.

•   •   •

What is this tale about? Greed, certainly. But the parable also shows how stubbornness and greed can keep people from embracing the goodness around them. It is never the greed itself that drives a person to despair, but a hardness of the heart, the fear of submission to life's inherent goodness.

We can never truly enjoy wealth unless the wealth itself has ceased to be the center of our desire. The greatest gift we can give ourselves is the joy of being released from passing fancies or meaningless pursuits.

7

Finding the Wisdom Within

O World, thou choosest not the better part!
It is not wisdom to be only wise,
And on the inward vision close the eyes,
But it is wisdom to believe the heart.

—George Santayana

Most religions, in addition to having ethical guidelines and ritualistic practices, also have one or more wisdom traditions. Sometimes a wisdom tradition emerges as a challenge to the historic understanding or the commonly accepted theology or practice of the faith—as is the case with Christianity and the Desert Fathers and, to a lesser extent, the wisdom traditions that are part of the Franciscan legends.

Judaism, likewise, has its wisdom traditions, as found in Proverbs, Ecclesiastes, and Job—traditions that bring a new light to the accepted theology of the Deuteronomic historian who collected a sizable portion of the early Hebrew Bible. Later Jewish wisdom traditions, such as the Hassidic tradition of the seventeenth century, sought, in part, to bring a new approach to the practice of the faith.

Zen Buddhism and Islamic Sufism could also be considered wisdom outcroppings from within their respective faiths.

But on another level, these various wisdom traditions offer a rich array of stories and parables for practical consideration. Here can be found stories of wisdom and foolishness, tales defining the extremes of human experience, and parables that point beyond themselves to higher truths.

As one Jewish parable illustrates, the wise are those who seek wisdom, and the fool is one who thinks wisdom has already been obtained:

> A Roman noblewoman approached the rabbi and asked, "What sense can be made from the saying: 'God gives wisdom to the wise'? Shouldn't it say: 'God gives wisdom to the foolish'?"
>
> The rabbi replied, "Do you have any jewelry?"
>
> "Yes," the noblewoman responded.
>
> "And if two people came to borrow your jewelry—one rich and the other poor—to whom would you lend your valuables?"
>
> "Oh," she replied, "to the one who is rich."
>
> "And why?"
>
> "Because the one who is rich would be able to pay for the jewels should they be lost or stolen. One who is poor, on the other hand, could not."
>
> "Likewise," the rabbi said, "God gives wisdom to the wise, and not to fools."

To find the wisdom within, we must open ourselves to the wisdom of the ages, and to the joys of learning. To be truly wise, as the sages say, is also to understand that our knowledge is limited. The beginning of wisdom, therefore, is to understand our need.

That Is What You Are
(Hindu)

There once lived a boy named Svetaketu. One day his father said to him, "It's time for you to become a student of sacred wisdom. After all, everyone in our family has studied the holy Vedas and so should you."

When the boy was twelve, he began his studies, then returned home when he was twenty-four, proud of his knowledge of the Vedas and possessing a high opinion of himself.

His father noticed this pride and said, "Svetaketu, I've noticed your arrogance. It's true—you've learned a lot—but have you asked for the knowledge that a person might hear that has not been heard before; or have you sought to think what has not been thought before; or do you try to perceive what has not been perceived?"

"What are you talking about?" asked the young man.

"Consider a lump of clay," the father said. "All that is clay can be known by a single word—'clay'—but the reality of clay is quite different. 'Clay' is clay! Or what about a nugget of gold? Gold, too, is known by the word 'gold,' but in reality, 'gold' is gold. Or if you had an iron cutter, you'd know what iron was when you felt it. But in reality, 'iron' is iron. You see, words and the realities they represent are not always the same."

The young man answered, "It's obvious my teachers didn't know this, otherwise they would have told me. Tell me more, Father."

So the father instructed his son in many things. He showed his son how food breaks down into three parts when it is eaten— waste, flesh, and mind. Likewise, he demonstrated how water is broken into three—as urine, blood, and breath.

The father also asked his son to fast for fifteen days. Afterwards, he asked his son many questions, but the young man could not recall the answers. "Yes," said the father, "and that is exactly how it is with the body. It is like a fire that has had one of its embers taken away. It seems insignificant at the time, but even a small ember diminishes the heat of the fire. Without food, your mind is diminished also."

Then the father asked his son to bring a piece of fruit from the banyan tree.

"Here it is," the son said.

"Break it open. Tell me what you see," said the father.

"I see very small seeds."

"Break one of the seeds open. Tell me what you see."

"I see nothing at all."

The father said, "From the very essence within the seed, which you cannot see, comes in truth the entire banyan tree. Likewise, the invisible is the Spirit of the entire universe. That is reality. That is the essence of what you are."

The son asked for more explanation.

"Very well," said the father. "Place some salt in water and come back tomorrow morning."

The next day his father told him, "Now bring me the salt you placed in the water."

The young man looked for the salt, but it had dissolved.

His father said, "Taste the water from the right side."

"It is salt," said the young man.

"Taste from the middle."

"It is salt."

"Taste from the left side."

"It is still salt."

"Now look for the salt again, and when you find it, come and tell me."

The young man studied the water for hours, but returned saying, "I cannot see the salt. I see only water."

"Yes," said the father. "And in the same way, you cannot see the Spirit. Yet the Spirit is here. This invisible essence is the Spirit of the entire universe. This is reality. This is truth. That is what you are."

The son asked for more explanation.

The father said, "Suppose there was a man who was blindfolded and taken to the desert. He would wander aimlessly and never arrive at his destination. But if this man met a good friend who removed the blindfold and told him where to find the land of the Gandharas, this same man would go from village to village and would inquire until he reached his destination. He would be wise to do this.

"And so it happens in this world that every person needs a master to direct him to the land of the Spirit. Such a person will say, 'I will wander this world until I have found freedom, and then I will go and reach my Home.'

"The unseen is the Spirit of the entire universe. That is reality. That is truth. That is what you are."

•   •   •

The philosophical traditions of the Hindu faith are to be found in the Upanishads, a massive collection of observations about life and death and the human condition. Written in a majestic poetic style, the Upanishads' primary teaching centers on Brahma, the Spirit that underlies and creates all things. Written between 800 B.C.E. and the fifteenth century C.E., these verses and poetic stories offer guidance and wisdom dealing with the entire spectrum of human experience.

This parable from one of the longest Upanishads—the Chandogya Upanishad—points to the need for truth seeking and offers a path for the spiritual seeker. As the parable teaches: The end of all things is to reach for and obtain the wisdom of what is unseen—the Spirit that underlies all things.

This in itself is the very meaning of the Sanskrit word Upanishad—which has to do with sitting at the feet of a master and learning. To listen and learn from those who have walked before us, according to the tradition, is the beginning of wisdom. As this parable teaches, learning to see what cannot be seen with the eyes, to hear what cannot be heard with the ears, and to understand what cannot be analyzed with the mind is the first step toward delighting in the Spirit.

∾

The Character of Leadership
(Confucian)

Tzu-kung once asked the Master about the three pillars of government. Confucius replied, "They are food, weapons, and the confidence of the people."

His friend asked, "Yet, suppose you had to forgo one of the three. Which is the most expendable?"

"Weapons," Confucius replied.

"And suppose you had to forgo one of the remaining two?"

"Food," Confucius answered. "For history has proven that death must come to all. But a people who no longer trusts its rulers is already lost."

•   •   •

Like many of the teachings of Confucius—perhaps the most famous moral teacher of the East, with the exception of Buddha—this bit of wisdom deals with the moral truths that form the foundation of human experience. Many Confucian teachings challenge our modern sensibilities and, unlike many religious teachers, Confucius guards his thoughts on spirituality—for he considered such things unknowable, and never speaks of God or immortality. Once, when asked about the nature of spiritual beings, Confucius responded, "If one cannot know people, how can one know spirits?"

Rather, Confucian wisdom centers on character and integrity, two characteristics needed to be a leader of people. The wisdom of Confucius may be found, not in his insistence that others revere or worship him, but in his gentle instruction on the destiny of humanity and the highest nature of our being. Confucius was born in 551 B.C.E. in the duchy of Lu, China, and died in 478 B.C.E., having earned the respect of his disciples and fellow citizens for his virtuous teaching and his contribution to the way of wisdom.

A Solid Foundation
(Buddhist)

There was a wealthy but foolish man who once envied a neighbor's three-story house. He hired a carpenter to build a replica of this house. The carpenter agreed and began the process of building the foundation, with plans to complete the second story and at last the third.

But when the wealthy man noticed this, he told the carpenter, "I am not worried about the foundation or the second story. Just build me the third story, and do not waste time."

•　　•　　•

The maxim still applies: Haste makes waste. Shortcuts typically lead to ruin and despair.

As with many Buddhist parables, this humorous story clearly demonstrates impatience and the destructive nature of envy. There is an art to waiting, and in life not all things come to those who work hard and demand results. Some of life's greatest triumphs and achievements are of the lifetime variety—when we look back over the span of many years and see what has been built, one step at a time.

Without a solid foundation to build on, no one can achieve the highest ideals of life. Every successful venture is built on a previous achievement. Every stage of life is built on the stage before. There are no shortcuts in life. It is only through persistence and patience that one reaches the highest levels of understanding and the grandest goals.

Be Prepared at All Times
(Parables of Jesus)

The kingdom of heaven is like this.

There were ten brides who were preparing for their weddings. Five were foolish and five were wise. The foolish brides did not put oil in their lamps when they prepared for their weddings. But the wise brides prepared flasks of oil with their lamps.

When the groom was delayed, all the brides became drowsy and fell asleep. But at midnight, the announcement came: "Get up! The groom is almost here. Get ready to meet him!"

Immediately all ten got up to meet the groom. However, the foolish brides were not prepared. They asked the wise brides, "Give us some of your oil. Our lamps are going out and it's getting dark."

The wise brides answered, "No. There will not be enough oil for you and us both. You'd better go buy oil for yourselves."

While the foolish brides were away, however, the groom came. He took the wise brides to the wedding party, and shut the door behind him. Later, when the foolish brides returned with their oil, they knocked on the door. "Open up," they said. But the groom replied, "I'm sorry, but I don't know you."

So keep awake, since you do not know the day nor the hour.

❧

Whoever hears these words of mine and lives them will be like a wise man who built his house on solid rock. Rains descended, floods came, and winds howled against that house, but it did not collapse because it was built on solid rock.

Whoever hears these words of mine and does not live by them will be like a foolish man who built his house on shifting sands. Rains descended, floods came, and the winds howled against that house. It collapsed in utter ruin.

•   •   •

Jesus was largely concerned with the approaching reign of God and the need for people to prepare for God's work. His many parables illustrate the need, on the part of his followers, to watch for this coming advent. Wisdom, according to Jesus, is centered on a faith that anticipates and creatively envisions what God is doing or will do. To miss God's advent in life is to miss the presence of joy, and might be compared to building one's life on a temporal foundation.

As with most of the parables of Jesus, one is challenged and invited to help usher in the kingdom of God. Although God is the One who reigns, people are invited to be participants in these mighty acts and to serve as witnesses.

These two parables open the kingdom to those who, by faith, build on the foundation of God's revelation through Jesus.

❧

A Box, a Cane, and a Pair of Shoes
(Buddhist)

Once there were two demons who were arguing over a box, a cane, and a pair of shoes. A man, who happened to be passing by, overheard this argument and stopped to inquire. "Why are you arguing over such trivial things?" he asked the demons.

They explained, "Well, the box might contain something we desire: food, clothing, or treasure. With the cane we can overpower all our enemies. And if we had those shoes, we could walk on air."

The man said, "But this is no way to settle an argument. If you go away for a few minutes and let me think, I will divide these things for you."

The two demons retreated. When they were out of sight, however, the man picked up the box and the cane, put on the shoes, and departed.

• • •

Bickering rarely settles disputes. Anger overpowers reason. And by the time the smoke clears from most arguments, someone else has walked off the battlefield carrying the spoils.

This parable reveals the absurdity of trivial arguments through the humorous escapades of spirits and people. Even among the most spiritually minded, we can see the bickering and rivalry that divides people. Having spiritual knowledge and insight is not the end of wisdom—but the beginning of learning through humility and gentleness.

Faith has little to do with what one believes. Rather, faith and depth of spiritual insight is demonstrated through how one lives and the good choices one makes day by day. In essence, it's not the big decisions that matter most, but being attentive to the small matters that others miss.

The symbolism found in this parable also points to the three areas of life people most desire: food, which represents the basic necessities of life; shoes, which represent freedom and the ability to move about; and a cane, which represents spiritual discernment and power.

To spend time worrying over these things, however, is to miss the opportunities for daily enjoyment.

❧

Two Wise Stories from Avianus
(Avianus)

A fisherman once caught a very small fish. The fish told him, "Throw me back. Can't you see that I'm too small? Release me to the lake again, allow me to grow, and a year from now, when you come back and catch me, I will make quite a meal for you. I suggest this as much for your self-interest as my own."

The fisherman shook his head and said, "Ah, yes. But you know the old saying: A bird in the hand is worth two in the bush."

"What do birds have to do with it? I'm no bird," said the fish.

"And I'm no fool," said the fisherman, who took the fish home, cleaned it and cooked it, and had himself a tiny mouthful of delight.

❧

A lark had made her nest in a field of wheat. There in the rustling shade of the wheat shafts, she raised her little ones.

One day, when the mother was away, the chicks overheard the farmer talking to his wife, saying, "It appears that harvest time has come. I'll ask my neighbors to give me a hand."

When the mother returned, the chicks told her what they had heard. "Pay no attention to these words," the mother said. "We have no need to fear the neighbors."

A few days later, when the mother was gone, the chicks again overheard the farmer saying, "The harvest has come. I will ask my friends to lend me a hand."

When the mother returned, the chicks told her what they had overheard.

"Pay no attention to these words," the mother said. "We have no reason to fear the farmer's friends."

Yet a few days later, the mother lark observed the farmer sitting alone on his porch, sharpening his reaping sickle. "Now it is time to leave," the mother bird explained. "The farmer has given up his dreams of receiving help from neighbors and friends, and will harvest the crop himself. Now is the time for us to fly away."

•　　•　　•

Some 900 years after the death of Aesop—the famed collector of Greek morality parables—a lyrical Latin poet by the name of Avianus began writing stories in metrical verse. Although many of these parables are ambiguous in meaning, there are, nevertheless, some gems in the collection.

The first parable demonstrates the wisdom of understanding our blessings and taking advantage of daily opportunities. It is all well and good to have big plans in life, but sometimes it is best for us to settle for smaller achievements. Otherwise, we run the risk of losing out on some encouraging accomplishments. Advice might also be good, but consider the source. Much advice in life is biased—and the wise person is the one who can discern truth through common sense and cautious observation.

The second parable teaches the valuable lesson of knowing the proper time and place for action. Not all opportunities in life are to be equally weighed. Those who cry destruction and despair are usually wrong. And in the end, we can determine the best plan of action by following the dictates of our senses and intelligent observation.

A Leaf from the Tree of Knowledge
(Yiddish)

There was a peasant who became lost in the desert and soon found himself in the middle of a violent sandstorm. So powerful were the winds that the peasant was whirled round and round; he was toppled head over heels. When the storm was over, the peasant found himself sitting on a pile of windblown junk, staring at a path leading to a village.

Now, as he walked along, a strange thing began to happen. The peasant discovered that his mind was clearer than it had ever been. He saw the world as he had never seen it before, and his thoughts resonated with wisdom. After some time, the peasant grew so weary from his lofty thoughts that he sat down to rest by removing his sandals.

However, as soon as he removed his sandals, he felt as foolish and ignorant as he had been before. As soon as he put his sandals back on, the wisdom returned. Believing that the sandals were the key to his knowledge, he continued on his journey.

Now, in reality, what had actually happened was that, during the sandstorm, a leaf from the Tree of Knowledge out of the Garden of Eden had become lodged on the bottom of one sandal.

When the peasant came to the village, he found that a king lived there. And as fate would have it, the king's daughter was dying of a dreadful disease.

Through some of the king's emissaries, the peasant sent word that he had a cure for the princess. Through his new-found wisdom, he invented a potion to cure the disease. A few days after taking the peasant's potion, the princess was entirely well.

Wanting to reward the peasant, the king invited him to the palace for a few days. But when the king saw that the peasant had the appearance of an ignorant man, he asked his royal physicians to determine if the peasant's remedy was real, or if it were merely magic.

After some days, the royal physicians returned to tell the king that the princess had fully recovered, and that the remedy was indeed based on wisdom and sound medicine.

The king asked the peasant, "What is the secret of your wisdom?"

"It's my sandals," the peasant said.

"Is this a joke?" the king asked.

The peasant assured the king that it was not. And soon afterward, the king offered the peasant half of his kingdom in exchange for the sandals—an exchange the peasant eagerly accepted.

Naturally, as soon as the king gained possession of the sandals, he asked his servants to give them a good washing, and during this washing, the leaf from the Tree of Knowledge fell off and was thrown away. So the king had new sandals, but no greater wisdom than before. The peasant, on the other hand, had half a kingdom.

•   •   •

What is this parable about? Perhaps it has to do with God's gifts of wisdom, or it may be a lesson about the strange twists of life.

After all, life is not fair. Some people are wise but have no material possessions or position to show for it. Others are fools but seem to rise to the top. Not even the wise can figure out why this is so, but it is human nature to believe that wealth is the result of superior knowledge or achievement. Often, however, it's just dumb luck!

❧

The Essence of Time
(Buddhist)

A man going on a long journey came to a river. He observed both sides and said to himself, "The other side looks better suited for walking. But how shall I get across?"

So he built himself a raft made of branches and hollow reeds. After crossing the river safely, he said to himself, "I've invested a lot of time building the raft. I can't simply leave it along the bank to rot. I'll have to carry it with me."

•   •   •

It is not wise to assume unnecessary burdens in life. Life is difficult enough, and there is no need to carry more than we can handle. Worry is one of the greatest of these unnecessary burdens, and the worry over material objects is one of the heaviest burdens many people carry.

Laying aside worry about material objects and possessions is one of the universal wisdoms shared in most religious traditions. And yet, this worry is often the one that plagues us the most.

As this little parable demonstrates, when we stop to consider the foolishness of such worry, it is actually humorous. After all, the entirety of our possessions and all that we have accumulated will eventually rot like the boat left along the bank of a river. The journey is paramount—not how much junk we can carry with us along the way.

❧

One Wise Meatball

(Native American/Comanche)

Many years ago a big meatball went rolling down the road. Soon he came upon a Coyote sitting beside a tumbleweed. "I am about to die of hunger," said the Coyote.

"All right," said Meatball, "take one big bite of me."

Coyote took a big bite and went on his way. He ran ahead of Meatball and sat down along the road again. When Meatball came along, Coyote said, "I am about to die of hunger."

Meatball said, "All right. Take one big bite of me."

Again Coyote went his way. He ran ahead of Meatball and sat down along the road. When Meatball came rolling along, Coyote said, "I am about to die of hunger."

Meatball studied Coyote closely. When Meatball was about to offer Coyote another bite, he saw meat stuck between Coyote's teeth.

"Aha!" said Meatball. "You are the same one who has been taking a bite out of me all along."

When Coyote realized he had been discovered, he ran away.

•   •   •

Some people are easy to understand. The wise are those who can see the self-seeking tendencies of others, and protect themselves from being placed at a disadvantage. Note that Coyote, like many people whose schemes are unmasked, flees the scene as soon as he is discovered.

Here is another piece of universal wisdom that can be found in many traditions and cultures. Just as Jesus warned his disciples to watch for those who wore sheep's clothing but inside were ravenous wolves, so this parable offers similar advice: watch out for those who plot to gain advantage through trickery and self-promotion.

There are also times, as this parable demonstrates, when the appearance of beggars can be deceiving. Sometimes—as this Mother Goose nursery rhyme reveals, there is more to a beggar than meets the eye.

Hark, hark, the dogs do bark,
The beggars are coming to town.
Some in rags, and some in tags,
And one in a velvet gown.

The Visitation
(Buddhist)

There was a man who dreamed of nothing but good fortune and wealth. One day a beautiful woman visited his house. The man asked who she was, and she replied, "I am the goddess of wealth."

Naturally, the fellow was very pleased to receive this news, and so he treated the woman kindly.

The next day there was another knock at the door. When the man answered, he found a very ugly woman on his steps, poorly dressed and eager to come in. "And who are you?" he asked.

"I am the goddess of poverty," the woman replied.

Quickly, the fellow tried to drive the woman away, but she refused to leave, saying, "The goddess of wealth is my sister. We have an agreement that we are never to live separately. Where one of us goes, the other follows. If you ask me to leave, my sister will depart with me."

Nevertheless, the man drove the goddess of poverty from his house. But when he went to look for the goddess of wealth, he discovered that she had departed as well.

• • •

Life is composed of opposites—forces that move and pull against one another. There are birth and death, fortune and misfortune, good and evil. Likewise, bad things follow good things, and good events frequently follow bad events.

It is foolish to believe we can experience only the good and forgo the bad. Life does not give us what we want just because we want it. Everyone, rich or poor, will experience a share of joy and heartache.

This parable is a reminder that wealth can never be an excuse to ignore poverty, nor can good fortune be considered a sanctuary from misfortune. All that is possessed can be lost. All that is lost can be found.

This is one of the basic teachings of Buddhist philosophy—that true enlightenment is gained when we learn to transcend both wealth and poverty and are free from all worldly attachments and desires.

Going to the Dogs
(Jewish)

A man was walking in the countryside by himself when suddenly he came upon a pack of wild dogs. Since he was afraid of them, he immediately sat down in their midst.

• • •

This short parable contains several truths about the nature of fear. First, to run away from our fears is to deny their existence, and may actually result in greater harm in the long run. But to remain calm in the midst of fear is the greatest testament to courage and results in peace.

It is also true that some fears are greatly magnified by number. Facing one person for a job interview, for example, is not as overwhelming as facing a room full of people. Regardless of how large our fears are, however, we can learn to bridle them, and we can find a peaceful center from which to make decisions.

Finally, there is much insight in the knowledge that other's fears may actually be greater than our own. Standing firm when others are ready to attack may actually disarm a threat and may lead to a peaceful resolution.

A Honey Pot of Wisdom
(Buddhist)

A fool was boiling honey in an open pot. When a friend stopped by, the fool wanted to offer his honey as refreshment, but it was too hot. Unwilling to remove the pot from the fire, the fool tried to fan the honey so it would be cool enough to serve.

•   •   •

The beauty and sweetness of life can rarely be savored when we are distracted by worry. It is easy to miss life's joys when our attention is focused on completing a job or trying to please someone.

Likewise, it is impossible to achieve two goals at the same time. A pot cannot be heated and cooled simultaneously, and we usually can't complete a job when other people are competing for our time and attention. Believing that we can achieve many goals at the same time is a foolish notion: learning how to prioritize is a sign of maturity.

The Fox and the Vineyard
(Jewish)

A hungry fox came upon a vineyard that was surrounded on all sides by fence. There was, however, a very narrow gap near one fence post. The fox tried to squeeze through this hole, but discovered he was too fat.

Since the fox didn't want a fence to get the better of him, he fasted for three days until he was lean and slender. Afterward, he had no difficulty squeezing through the narrow gap.

Entering the vineyard, the fox ate his fill of the grapes, but afterward discovered that he had grown too fat to exit through the fence. Again the fox fasted for three days until he grew lean and slender.

As soon as he squeezed through the fence, however, he realized he was hungry. Looking back at the vineyard, the fox thought to himself, "Yes, the vineyard is full of good fruit. But what benefit can I derive from it? If I enter it to consume the goodness, I must also deprive myself of the same goodness."

• • •

Here is a parable with some common sense. Everyone knows that most things are not as exciting as they first appear. As with most good things, there can be a hook attached if the gift is used wrongly.

One common device used in many Jewish parables is the use of animal characters to reveal the foibles and weaknesses of human practice and thought. The parable demonstrates that it is never wise to devise a plan without considering the ramifications and the steps one will need to take to achieve the goal. Much of human failure and suffering is produced by shortsighted strategies and quick fixes. The initial goal may be easily achieved or acquired, but delivering the final results may prove disastrous or, at best, land us in the same circumstances we faced at the beginning.

Better to wait for the next opportunity than to waste time and energy focusing on lost causes.

On the other hand—and in Jewish wisdom there is always the other hand!—it is necessary to note that some ends require us to use ingenuity and cunning to acquire what we need. The result might not be a long-term solution but might provide what is needed for a short time.

The Success of the Three Maestros
(Taoist)

Three accomplished experts—a harpist, a piano tuner, and a philosopher—each wanted to teach. All three had achieved recognition in their respective fields of knowledge and were quite famous in their time. But when they began to teach, they attempted to explain what they did not understand and ended up their lives in obscurity. They were able to pass along their expertise only to their children. In this manner their influence came to an end.

Now if this is success, who has not been successful?

If this is not success, then no one has been successful.

•   •   •

Anyone who presumes to teach others must proceed with caution. Teaching is difficult. Knowledge changes. What passes for brilliance one day may become ancient philosophy the next. And a body of knowledge is only as good as the teaching methods of the expert. Sometimes it is best to practice an area of knowledge rather than to try and pass it along to someone else.

As the parable concludes, however, there is also an element of success in teaching one's children. This is the most profound influence a person can have in life.

It is good to remember that the greater the number one is trying to teach, the greater the odds that one will fail.

The Talking Skull
(African)

A hunter went into the bush and found a human skull. The hunter asked, "What brought you here?" The skull replied, "Talking brought me here."

Overwhelmed with his find, the hunter ran to tell the king. When the king heard the story he said, "Never in my life have I heard of a talking skull." He summoned his wise men and asked them about this oddity. But none of them had heard of a talking skull, either.

So the king summoned one of his guards and said, "Go with this hunter into the bush. Find the skull. If it talks, bring it back to me. If the hunter is lying, kill him."

The hunter and the guard went into the bush and found the skull. The hunter said, "What brought you here, skull?" But the skull was silent. So the guard killed the hunter on the spot.

After the guard departed, the skull opened its mouth and asked the dead hunter, "What brought you here?"

"Talking brought me here," the hunter replied.

•   •   •

Too much talk at the wrong time or with the wrong people can prove disastrous. A quick word is often regretted later, and given the choice between too much speech or too little, it is always wiser to choose the latter. Silence, as they say, is truly golden.

This is one of the most widely told African parables, common in most parts of Africa, and it is a wonderful example of African storytelling at its finest.

The Wisdom of Crows
(Japanese)

A flock of crows gathered in the woods to teach their fledglings how to fly. Each was put to the test with a single question: "What, in your estimation, should we fear the most?"

The first fledgling answered, "An arrow." The older birds flapped their wings in approval and the parents puffed with pride. "You are one of us now," the crow council said.

A second fledgling gave its response. "I believe the archer is more terrifying than the arrow itself. For without someone to shoot the arrow, it is a harmless thing."

"Most true! Most true!" the crow council cawed. "You also are accepted into our ranks."

The third fledgling spoke up. "I think neither answer is correct."

"What?" asked the council, ruffling their feathers.

"It is not the archer with skill who is to be feared," the young crow answered. "For a skillful archer always shoots true, and we can therefore judge where to fly to elude the arrow. But an unskilled archer has no aim. His arrow may fly to the left or the right of its target. Where skill is lacking, there is far greater danger."

When the council heard this answer, they were astounded. Everyone bowed in humility before the youngster and he was appointed the new leader of the crow council.

• • •

Those who know what they are doing are not nearly as frightening as those who are ignorant, or who have little regard for others. It is not the contemplative sniper who is to be feared, but the fellow next door who is angry and out of control. The parable demonstrates that we should be wary of those who might do harm. It is best to keep a safe distance.

Likewise, it is wise to educate those who might lack knowledge. By giving others knowledge, we offer empowerment and might actually save a life. There is far greater possibility for harmony if people have common values and a sense of equality.

The Reminder
(Aesop)

A farmer's child was playing near a snake's den. The poisonous snake bit the child, and the child died. The farmer, overcome with grief and anger, took his ax and set up a vigil outside the snake's den. When the snake poked its head out, the farmer swung the ax, but missed, splitting a rock in half instead. At this point, the farmer thought it would be best to make peace with the snake. But the snake replied, "There can never be peace between us as long as there are visible reminders of our past. I will always see the split rock. You will always see your child's tombstone."

• • •

What makes peace difficult to accomplish, particularly between peoples and nations, are the visible reminders of past conflicts. It is nearly impossible to draw up a peace accord while bomb craters still pockmark the ground. Peaceful conversation is painful as long as the memories of past injuries and lies are easily recalled. Reconciliation usually comes about long after the bullets have stopped flying and those who were initially involved in the conflict are gone.

Perhaps, as this insightful parable explains, we must first remove all vestiges of past conflicts before beginning a discussion of reconciliation. We can never truly forget an injury, but it helps to rid ourselves of the daily reminders.

The World and More
(Taoist)

It has been said: Nothing in the world is larger than the tip of a hair; even a huge mountain is small. Another parable: No one lives longer than the one who dies as a child; a person who lives eight hundred years is young. All of heaven and earth are born when we are born; all living things are one with us. If all is one, then what else can be said? And once it has been said that all is one, how can more be expressed?

• • •

A classic Taoist parable, this teaching asks us to consider the eternal in the transient, the universal in the particular. Such thoughts may seem very odd to Western minds, but the idea is that one can never fully explain the substance of a thing by its appearance, and one can find the past and future contained in a single moment.

In Jewish and Christian thought, perhaps the closest teachings come from Jesus, who spoke of the kingdom of God being within, and once asked his disciples to become as children. Eternity is not a reality that lies beyond, but one that is experienced and contained in the here and now.

Personal Perspective
(Jewish)

Two sages were sitting at the fire debating a controversial question: From which end does a person grow? The first insisted that any fool could see that a person grows from the bottom up.

"What proof do you have?" insisted the second.

"Just this," answered the first. "Several years ago I bought myself this pair of pants. They were so long the cuffs dragged the ground. Now look at them! See how short they have become. What other proof do you need?"

"Doesn't prove a thing," insisted the second. "It's obvious that a person grows from the head up. Why just the other day I was watching a parade of soldiers. It was obvious from watching that they were all equal at the feet. Only their heads differed in height."

• • •

As is the case with this humorous parable, Jewish wisdom can often find meaning in a foolish debate. Perhaps the tale reminds us that one's perspective has a great deal to do with how one understands a situation or a question. If one is looking high, it is tough to see the position of the one who is looking low. Either way, a well-rounded perspective considers all the nuances of an argument. Perhaps it is not *where* one is looking that makes the difference, but *how* one looks.

Appearances Can Be Deceiving
(Taoist)

While on a journey, Tzu-ch'i noticed a huge tree in the distance. Tzu-ch'i said, "What a unique tree. No doubt it has enormous potential."

But when he came closer, he noted that the limbs were too crooked to be used as beams and the roots were too rotten to be used as coffins. Tasting a leaf, he discovered the foliage was bitter and emitted a terrible odor.

Tzu-ch'i then realized why the tree had grown so large: it was useless.

•   •   •

Often it is not the outward appearance of a thing that determines its value. One must also consider the unseen factors and the potential of the object. Judgments based on appearance alone can lead to difficulties later on.

The parable also points out a universal truth. Some things achieve the appearance of grandeur and importance because they are essentially useless. Some people rise to the top through continual failure. Some achieve fame and fortune by highlighting their odd idiosyncrasies and nastiness.

What most long for, however, is a sense of usefulness. It is better to have others regard us with fondness than to think of us as shallow and bitter.

The Snake and the Treasure
(Jewish)

One day a man was walking through a field with a jug of milk in his hand when a snake met him, moaning with thirst. "Why are you moaning?" asked the man. The snake replied, "Because I am thirsty. Please tell me what it is you carry in your hand."

"Milk," the man said.

The snake groaned. "Give me the milk to drink and I promise to show you more money than you can imagine."

When he heard this, the man gave his milk to the snake and it drank freely.

"Now show me the money," the man demanded.

"Follow me," said the snake, leading the fellow through the field until they came to a gigantic stone. The snake pointed to the rock and said, "The money is hidden beneath this boulder."

The man dug around the stone, lifted it slightly, and discovered a stash of money. The fellow was surprised to find what the snake had promised. But as soon as the man took the money the snake coiled itself around his throat. "Why are you doing this?" the fellow gasped.

"I'm going to kill you because you took all the money," said the snake. "It's rightfully mine."

The man gasped, "No. Wait. Come with me to Solomon's court so he may decide between us."

And so they went to appear before Solomon, with the snake still coiled around the man's neck. The fellow made his appeal to the king. Then Solomon turned to the snake and asked, "And what do you have to say about this?"

"I just want to kill him," hissed the snake.

"Release your hold from his throat," Solomon demanded. "Since you are both in court, it is not right for you to have control of him while he has no control of you." The snake released its hold and slithered onto the ground.

Solomon said, "Now tell me what you have to say in your defense."

The snake said, "I wish to kill the man in keeping with what the Holy One said to me: 'You shall strike him in the heel.'"

Solomon said to the man, "And the Holy One has commanded you, 'You are to strike him on the head.'" At that word the man immediately sprang upon the snake and smashed its head.

•　　•　　•

This parable, of course, has nothing to do with snakes and money, but everything to do with power, corruption, and justice. Wisdom tells us that if we are going to do business with a snake, it is best to protect ourselves in the event that the snake turns on us later. Business deals are best conducted among people who can be trusted.

The court scene also reveals another truth. When power is unequal, some power must be relinquished before truth can be established and justice meted out. A corporate executive has an unequal balance of power over those who work for the company. A teacher has more authority than a student. A police officer has more authority than a citizen behind the wheel. It is tough for the person of lesser power to issue a complaint against a superior or file a suit for justice. But to do so shows courage and conviction. Justice can only be meaningful on a level playing field.

❧

A Big Fish in a Small Pond
(Taoist)

Prince Jen created an enormous fishhook, baited it with fifty bulls, and settled himself on top of a mountain to cast into the sea. Each morning he dropped his line in the water but caught nothing. He fished for a year without success.

Then one day a gigantic fish took the bait. Prince Jen set the hook deep and battled the fish in a ferocious struggle. The fish dove to the depths, rose to the surface in a mighty charge, and shook its fins in an attempt to rid itself of the hook. Prince Jen prevailed, however, and when he landed the fish, he cut it into a thousand pieces, dried it in the sun, and gave everyone for miles around a piece to eat.

Since that time, sages of far less talent have tried to appease each other by retelling this story. It was as if they baited their poles with minnows and went to fish in tiny rivulets and streams. Of course, they never landed a big fish.

Take care that you do not parade around your little fish, or you will be far from the Great Understanding.

•   •   •

This parable, from the classical writings of Chuang-tzu, is a marvelous bit of wisdom. If you want to achieve something great in life, you must think and act *big*! Success may be longer in coming—and the temptation is always to settle for a quick fix or a smaller catch—but the end result will be grand.

What is needed for the big payoff? As the story suggests, preparation and patience are key elements. The prince came loaded for a great struggle, sat for a year without success, then landed a whopper! Those who try to repeat the performance, of course, pale by comparison to the one who accomplishes the feat first. We don't, after all, typically remember who climbed Mount Everest second, or who got to the North Pole in third place.

Finally, the parable offers a strong caution. Beware of parading smaller accomplishments as if they were giant achievements. The Great Understanding is none other than humility—the one virtue that makes great achievements possible. Those who are meek may indeed inherit the earth.

8

Seeing the Possibilities

*The great thing in this world is not so much where we are,
but in what direction we are moving.*

—Oliver Wendell Holmes

The universe, we've discovered, is a very big place! And our little corner of it—this home we call earth—is over-flowing with beauty, wonder, and potential. The possi-bilities, of course, are endless.

It's sometimes difficult, however, for people to imagine what could be.

Consider, for example, the Egyptian scribe mentioned in Walter Jackson Bates's book, *The Burden of the Past*. This short-sighted scribe, who lived four thousand years ago, wrote sorrow-fully of the lack of fresh ideas and new insights. According to this scribe, all worthy phrases had already been used by "those of old," and, therefore, there were no more good books that could be written, no fresh perspectives that writers could use to express their thoughts or describe the world.

This idea seems ludicrous, of course, as we now look back four thousand years and see that most of the greatest works of literature were yet to be composed: the works of Homer, Aris-totle, and Shakespeare, plus the Bible, the Koran, and thousands of other classics, had not yet been written.

And yet, we must admit that our vision of the future is but a dim image of what the future will actually be.

Seeing the possibilities in life means that we are able to look beyond what *is* and see what *might be*. True visionaries are *how* thinkers, not *if* thinkers. Or, as author Stanley Arnold once said: "Every problem contains the seeds of its own solution."

Finding the answers to life's difficulties may not always come from a bigger bank account, or a better government, or even from a religious institution. Sometimes, answers are found within—perhaps in a stronger self-confidence, a deeper faith, or a willingness to work with others.

Vision may be what is lacking, but vision and imagination are the keys to unlocking the greatest possibilities of the future. Without vision there is no direction. And without direction, there is no journey, but merely a haphazard wandering through life.

The parables in this chapter offer fresh perspectives on life, new ways of looking at old problems, and twisted thinking that arrives at surprising conclusions. The stories here may offer something for individuals and communities, but they will challenge and inspire.

Possibilities are not far off. Rather, they are close at hand. Dreamers may not always achieve their dreams, but no great dream was ever accomplished without a dreamer. Thomas Carlyle, the well-known Scottish essayist and historian, once summed this up eloquently: "Our grand business in life is not to see what lies dimly at a distance, but to do what lies clearly at hand."

Hurry Up and Wait
(Zen Buddhist)

A certain devotee had a reputation for zeal and dedication. He neither ate nor drank, and he spent his entire time in the temple praying. As time went by, however, he grew thin and weak.

The temple master went to see him and said, "I advise you to be more patient in your efforts. Please take better care of yourself."

The devotee responded, "But I am after enlightenment."

"Why are you rushing?" the master asked. "What is your hurry?"

"There is no time to waste."

"And how do you know," asked the master, "that this enlightenment is not right in front of you, while you are rushing ahead to find it? Perhaps it lies behind you, and you must stand still."

•   •   •

Patience is one of the keys to achieving any dream. Hard work and effort also play a part, but endurance and time will make up for many personal shortcomings and mistakes. Learning to wait is one of the most difficult lessons, but rest and recreation are vitally important for improving focus, sharpening the senses, and renewing the spirit.

The deepest knowledge is not always obtained through study, but sometimes through observation and listening. The greatest achievements are not always the result of intense effort, but sometimes come about through relaxation and focus.

A Better Life
(Jewish)

Once upon a time there was a husband and wife who were blessed with twin sons. But from the very beginning, it was obvious that one of the sons was clever and the other foolish.

As a child, the foolish son would often sit around the house, daydreaming and eating. He rarely ventured beyond the yard and was quite ignorant of the ways of the world. It seemed to his parents that they would always have him underfoot, and they worried about his future.

The clever son, however, was the pride and joy of his parents. He studied Torah daily, had many friends, and was eager to see the world and make his mark.

When the brothers grew old enough to be on their own, the clever brother looked around the house one day and realized that his parents had made many sacrifices. They were not destitute, exactly, but they were by no means wealthy. Why, it was a struggle just to prepare a decent Passover meal. And there was rarely enough for a celebration with the neighbors.

But the foolish brother continued to sit around the house and eat, rarely lifting a finger to help his struggling parents.

"Enough of this," the clever brother told his parents one day. "I'm old enough to go out into the world and seek my fortune. My first order of business will be to make enough money so that we can repair the house, buy new clothing, and begin to live a bit. We'll have the best Passover meal ever."

When the parents saw that their clever son was indeed ready to go into the world, they hugged him and kissed him and loaded him up with the best things they could find— biscuits, fruit, butter, and enough bread for the journey. They gave him what little money they had saved, and the father and mother offered their advice: "Beware of others. They will try to take advantage of you. Be wise and don't do anything that we wouldn't do."

And with that word the clever brother struck out into the world. He left the town of his childhood and was soon walking in the countryside, eager to make his fortune.

He had not been gone long, however, when a dog came running up the road toward him. The dog was mangy and matted; it was covered with dirt and smelled of dung. The clever brother was much surprised when the dog spoke. "Dear sir," the dog said, "I beg you to clean me up. Wash me and comb me and give me something to eat and I promise to repay you some day."

The clever brother remembered, however, what his parents had told him. "What kind of a fool do you think I am?" he told the dog. "My father would never clean and feed a dog like you, nor my mother either. Get out of here!"

So the dog ran away.

The clever brother went on a bit farther, feeling by now the heat of the day, and was much relieved when he came upon a well. When he peered inside the well, however, he noticed that a green scum floated on the surface of the water and there was mud everywhere. A silver cup hung on a nail over the well, but it was tarnished. The brother was so repulsed by the sight of the well, that his thirst left him immediately.

But suddenly the well spoke to him: "Dear sir, I beg you to clean me up. Brush away the scum from my surface, scrub my handle, polish the silver cup, and then you may drink. And someday I promise to reward you."

The clever brother was not to be tricked, however. "What kind of a fool do you think I am?" he told the well. "My father would never drink from a well like you, nor my mother either. Away with you!"

And so he journeyed on.

Just a few miles up the road, the clever brother spied a pear tree. Its branches were dry and withered and the roots of the tree had long been exposed to the elements and were rotting. There was not a pear to be found on the tree.

Suddenly the pear tree spoke. "Dear sir," it said, "I beg you to tend to my needs. Bring some water and pour it around my trunk. Cover my exposed roots with dirt, and I promise to reward you some day."

Again the clever son was not to be tricked. "What kind of a fool do you think I am?" he told the pear tree. "My father wouldn't take the time to water and nurture a tree like you, nor my mother either. Forget it!"

And with that word, he continued on his way.

A day later he came to a city and began to look for employment. There seemed to be few jobs, but the clever brother was eager to make his mark in the world. He went to an inn and asked the owner for a job.

"I can do most anything," he explained to the owner. "I'm a clever fellow who will work hard. Better yet, I won't even ask you for any wages. When my time of service has been completed, I will leave my payment to your sense of fairness."

The owner of the inn, seeing that the fellow was indeed eager to work, and hearing that he would work for no wages, hired him immediately. "You'll work for me an entire year," the owner said. "I'll provide your food and board, and after that time, if you have proven yourself true to your word, I'll reward you with a proper settlement."

For an entire year the clever brother worked for the innkeeper. He swept floors, cooked in the kitchen, carted trash, and even emptied the chamber pots. He mopped and dusted and scoured pans in the kitchen.

At the end of the year the owner was pleased, and the clever brother asked for his payment.

"Well," the owner told him, "I can't give you money, but I can give you something better. You're a clever fellow. Go out to my stable and look around. You'll see horses and wagons—some new and some old. Take what you like. You'll also see several chests—some large and some small. Choose from among these. When you have selected what you like, I bid you well as you return home to your parents."

The clever brother thanked his employer and ran to the stable. He was amazed at what he found. In the stable there were old horses and new, large chests and small, just as the innkeeper had said. So he quickly went about selecting the finest-looking things. He chose the best and strongest horse and the sturdiest wagon, and loaded it to the brim with the largest chests. He left the city with a sizable haul of goods and set out for home.

Not far down the road he spied a pear tree that was loaded with delicious-looking pears. The tree was large and full, with roots that seemed to burrow deep into the earth. Hopping off the wagon, the clever brother pulled down a branch to pluck himself a pear, but the branch quickly snapped back into place.

"Away with you," said the tree. "Earlier, when I asked you to water me, to tend to my branches and roots, you would have nothing of it. And now you have returned to pick my pears. Be gone!"

Seeing that he would get no pears from the tree, the clever brother plopped himself into the wagon and headed down the road again. Soon he came to a bright and sparkling well.

"Oh, my," he thought. "I'll just have myself a little drink."

Scurrying to the well, he peered down into the sweet-looking water. Reaching for the sparkling silver cup that hung on the nail nearby, he could almost taste the water on his lips when the well spoke to him. "Away with you!" the well said.

"Earlier, when I asked you to clear away the moss and dirt and to shine my silver cup, you would have nothing of it. And now you have returned to drink my water. Away with you!"

Again the clever brother plopped himself into the wagon and headed down the road. As he approached the outskirts of his hometown, he saw a dog running toward him. This dog was a sight to behold—healthy, clean, and beautifully combed. On its neck was a collar filled with pearls, rubies, and diamonds.

Scurrying from his wagon again, the clever brother called out to the dog. "Here, dog! Here, dog!" he cried. The dog ran to his side, but when the brother leaned over to remove the collar from the dog's neck, the animal said, "Away with you! Earlier, when I asked you to care for my mange, when I asked you to clean me up and comb my fur, you would have nothing of it. And now you have returned to take my collar. Begone!"

And with that word the dog ran away, barking all the way to town.

Perplexed and bewildered, the clever brother plopped himself into the wagon again and set off for town. But when he arrived at his old home, it was already late and everyone had gone to bed. The brother pounded on the door and windows of the home, shouting, "Father, Mother, get up, get up! It is your son. I have returned home with a fortune. Open the door, clear a table, and I will empty out my chests for you!"

His parents nearly sprang from their beds. They were overjoyed to see that their son was home and had returned with so many fine and wonderful things.

They called out to the neighbors, "Come and see! Come and see what our clever son has brought for us!"

They turned on the lights and cleared a table. Then they helped their son carry in his chests from the wagon. Everyone gathered around to see what was inside the chests.

But as soon as the clever son emptied out the chests, the sun came up and suddenly the beautiful horse turned into an old mare, the strong and able wagon changed into a rickety cart with splintered sides and lopsided wheels, and the fine-looking chests were nothing but musty old boxes.

The clever son was speechless. Finally he said, "Quick, empty out the boxes and look inside. They are filled with treasures beyond your wildest dreams—gold, silver, and precious stones."

But when the parents opened the boxes and turned them over, nothing came out but a couple of rats, a few mice, and a pile of dirt.

The mother wept. And the father began to scold his son. "What sort of trick is this?" he demanded to know. "You go away for a year to make your way in the world and you return with a pile of worthless junk."

All of the friends and neighbors laughed and returned to their homes.

But the foolish brother, who had been watching all of this from the very beginning, said, "Don't be angry with my brother. It isn't his fault. Let me go out into the world to make my mark. I will return with enough to last us a good, long while."

When the parents heard this, they nearly laughed. The father said, "Our clever son has been gone for a year and has returned with nothing. And now you want to try your luck in the world?"

But the foolish son continued to press his parents until, at last, they granted their permission. "Let's see what he can do," his mother insisted.

"Yes," said his father. "Perhaps a fool can have more luck."

The next morning the parents and the clever brother prepared a sack of provisions for the foolish brother, and off he went into the world to seek his fortune.

The foolish brother had no sooner gone beyond the outskirts of town when he came upon a mangy old dog that was encrusted with sores, filthy from head to foot. "Oh, kind sir," the dog said, "I beg you to clean me up. Wash me and comb me, give me something to eat and drink, and I promise to reward you some day."

The foolish brother didn't even think twice. He untied his sack, gave the dog a biscuit, and even let the wretched animal drink from his canteen. Then he washed the dog, rinsed him, and combed him until he was sleek and shiny. He rubbed a little ointment on the dog's mange and then went on his way, eager to make his fortune.

A bit farther up the road, the foolish brother came upon a well. Since he was dry and weary from his walking, he could almost taste the water on his lips. But when he came to the well, he noticed that it was covered with scum and was filled with dirt. A tarnished silver cup hung on a nail nearby.

Suddenly the well spoke up and said, "Kind, sir, I beg you to clean me up. Rake the scum from my surface and polish up my silver cup. If you do, I promise to reward you some day."

The foolish son didn't even think twice. He went to work on the dirty well—cleaning and scouring and polishing until the entire well—and its water—was brilliant. As soon as he finished, he was on his way again, eager to make his fortune.

Next he came to a tree with withered branches. The leaves looked dry and the branches were so barren that not a single pear could be found anywhere. The tree's roots were dry and brittle from having been exposed to the elements.

Suddenly the tree spoke. "Oh, kind sir," it said, "I beg you to water my roots and cover them with dirt. Prune my branches. If you do, I promise to reward you some day."

The foolish brother didn't even think twice. He went to his knees and began rooting in the soil, covering up the roots. Then he watered the tree heavily. Finally, he pruned back a few of the worst-looking branches and then set off down the road, eager to make his fortune.

Many miles later, he came to a city and went about the task of looking for a job. When none could be found, he finally went to an inn and asked the owner for a job. "I'll work for nothing," the foolish brother said. "And after a year, you can pay me whatever you think is fair."

The innkeeper accepted the brother's offer, gave him room and board, and set him to work. The foolish brother mopped the floors. He worked in the kitchen as a cook and even scoured the pots and pans afterwards. He swept and dusted and did laundry.

At the end of a year, the foolish brother came to the owner and said, "I've kept my part of the bargain. Now you give me what you owe."

The innkeeper said, "I can't pay you anything. But I can give you something much better. In back of the inn I have a stable. You may help yourself to whatever you find. I have young horses and old, good wagons and bad ones, and chests which are large and small. Take whatever you like as your pay and return home safely to your parents."

The foolish brother ran to the stable and found that the innkeeper had not lied. There were old horses and young horses, good wagons and bad ones, and chests of every size.

The foolish brother looked around and thought, "The innkeeper isn't a bad man. He trusted me. He gave me lots of work to do. I won't betray him by taking the best of his things."

So the brother went about the business of choosing his payment. He took the oldest horse—an old mare that was near death. He took the shabbiest wagon—which was almost falling apart. And he chose the smallest and dingiest chests— ones that nearly fell apart at the touch and were as light as feathers. Then he loaded his payment into the wagon, and set off for home. As he left the city, people laughed at him and said, "Now there goes a fool. He has chosen the worst things for his payment. For only a fool would work for a year and leave the city with such worthless things."

Not far down the road, however, the brother came upon a bright and beautiful tree loaded with golden pears. The branches of the tree spanned the road and hung heavy with fruit. The pears looked so delicious, and so he stopped and said, "Kind tree, I am hungry and weary, may I pluck a pear from your branches and eat?"

The tree answered, "Yes, friend. Take as many as you like. For you were the one who pruned back my old branches, watered my trunk, and covered my roots with soil."

The foolish brother ate but one pear, however, and didn't dare take more than he could eat. Then he thanked the tree and drove off again with his old mare and rickety wagon.

In a little while, he came to a sparkling well shimmering with sunlight. A shiny silver cup hung from a nail nearby. The fool was thirsty and parched from his journey and so he stopped for a drink. He peered into the well and discovered that it was full of bright, clear water.

He was about to take a drink when he stopped to ask the well, "May I take your silver cup and drink from your water? I've had a long journey and feel the heat of the day."

As soon as the well heard the foolish brother's voice, it answered, "Take the silver cup and drink all that you want. For you were the one who raked the moss from my surface, cleaned me up, and polished my silver cup. In fact, after you drink, please keep the silver cup as a reward."

This time the foolish brother kept the cup and plopped himself down in his wagon. As he headed down the road, he was unaware that his old horse seemed to walk with more energy and the wagon was actually beginning to gleam. The sun shone brightly and the foolish brother started to whistle a familiar song.

As he went along, a dog came running alongside the wagon. It was a lovely pet, well-groomed and manicured, with a coat that glistened in the sun. Around its neck was a collar studded with pearls, rubies, and diamonds.

The foolish brother called out to the dog and it leapt into the wagon, its tail circling in a sign of friendship. It recognized the foolish brother immediately.

"Kind sir," it said. "Please take my collar as your reward. For you were the one who cleaned me up. You were the one who put ointment on my mange, washed me, and combed my fur. You also fed me and let me drink from your canteen."

The foolish brother thanked the dog and removed the collar from the dog's neck. Then he drove toward home with his wagon loaded with an abundance of goods.

When he came to his hometown, however, it was late, and everyone was asleep. He pounded on the door and the windows and shouted, "Mother, Father! Come here and see what I have brought. Clear off a table so that I might empty out my chests."

When the parents realized that their foolish son had returned, they did not get up right away. "After all," they thought, "he is a foolish boy. What could he possibly have that would be of any value? Better to get a little more sleep."

After some time, however, the parents grew weary of their son knocking on the door. They arose from bed and cleared off a table. Then the parents and the clever brother helped the fool unload his wagon of goods.

This time, however, when the chests were opened, gold and silver came pouring out. There were diamonds and pearls, rubies and other precious stones. There was a silver cup and large mounds of ripe, juicy pears.

The mother hugged and kissed her son. The father invited all of the neighbors to his home for a celebration and was already making plans for the next Passover. Then he shook his head and said, "Now which of the two is the clever one and who is the fool?"

•   •   •

Wealth, friendship, and good fortune are always nearby, but these rewards do not always go to the wise and the hard-working. Life is rarely fair, and often the best of life comes to those who have the most luck, rather than the most brains. Being in the right place at the right time, knowing someone of influence, or falling headlong into a gold mine may all lead to a better life. Or sometimes good fortune comes, not as a result of planning, but as a result of having made certain choices.

The humor in this story reminds us that even fools have a chance to make something of themselves. Sometimes the prize does not go to the swiftest, the wisest, or the strongest, but to the luckiest or the most persistent.

Though this parable is most commonly associated with a Passover theme, it truly is a tale for all seasons. Here is a reminder that the future is not ascertainable to human beings. All one can do is live to the best of one's ability, be kind, and take advantage of the best and brightest opportunities when they present themselves.

In Retrospect
(Jewish)

A famous rabbi was sitting with some friends.

"When I was a young man," the rabbi said, "I was on fire. I wanted to grab everyone by the shoulders, shake them, and convince them that I had the truth. I prayed to God that I would have the wisdom and strength to change the world.

"When I reached mid-life I looked back and realized I had changed no one. The world was still the same. So I prayed to God that I would be given the wisdom and strength to change those around me who needed to see the truth.

"Ah, but now I am old and my prayer is much simpler. 'God,' I pray, 'at least give me the wisdom and strength to change myself.' "

•   •   •

What a simple concept, and yet so profound: change begins within. If we want others to be more kind and forgiving, we must be kind and forgiving ourselves. If we desire to see more generosity from others, we ourselves must be generous. If we hope to reconcile others, bring peace to the world, and inspire strength, we must be reconciled, be at peace with others, and be strong.

There are many things about this world we cannot change. There are some problems that are far too large for any one pair of hands, one voice, or one vision.

Sometimes people believe that they can make someone behave a certain way, or think a certain thought, or live a certain kind of life. Parents may make this mistake with their children. Religious leaders can fall into this trap, as can business leaders and teachers. To believe that one can have this type of far-reaching influence and power over others is arrogance.

One can, however, have a great effect on others by living an exemplary life. If we desire to see changes in others, we must first be willing to change ourselves. This is the most difficult challenge we face in life, but also the greatest achievement.

The Last of the Golden Eggs
(Aesop)

A farmer had a plump hen that laid some golden eggs. Believing the hen to be full of gold, the farmer killed the hen and looked inside its belly. He found that its innards were just like those of other hens. Thus, the farmer deprived himself of even the small profit he could have had.

•   •   •

Another classic from the Greek storyteller with a clear lesson: greed and impatience lead to wasted opportunities. Possibilities may lie within, but the wise person is one who waits patiently for results, and takes the profit as it comes.

A Greater Reward
(Buddhist)

A diver went into the sea to gather pearls. But as soon as he descended, he discovered a strong current. Jagged coral cut at his flesh. A vicious shark swam nearby, looking to attack.

The diver endured these perils, however, and obtained a pearl of rare beauty.

Likewise, a hermit desired to climb a high mountain. In order to train for what lay ahead, he practiced throwing his body against swords, he walked through fire, he endured great pain.

At last he climbed the mountain and found there a cool, refreshing breeze.

•   •   •

These two parables point to the same truth: that the highest achievements in life can only be obtained through perseverance, sacrifice, or great effort. The possibility of a greater reward, however, is enough to keep one motivated and striving. But one must remain focused on the goal.

In Buddhist tradition, these stories point to enlightenment— the state of being where one has transcended the physical and has found the refreshing breeze of pure being. But the stories might also illustrate the relationship between preparation and focus, and eventual success.

The lesson is simply this: if we desire to reach a lofty goal, we will achieve it only after much pain and sacrifice.

❧

The Nightingale and the Peacock
(Sufi)

The nightingale once offered this insight to the peacock: "When I sing, people listen to the beauty of my voice. This proves that people are not murderers but are interested in aesthetics."

The peacock considered this insight and decided to seek out an admiring throng of people. He found a large group of people and immediately began to prance about, folding and unfolding his colorful feathers.

One of the people said, "Look at that poor peacock strutting about. How unusual! There must be something wrong with it."

And so a few men seized the peacock and killed it, just to be certain the disease would not spread to the other domestic birds.

•　　•　　•

Gaining the attention of others is not always a good thing. Sports figures, politicians, and celebrities have learned the hard way that attention is not easy to handle. Those in the limelight have a tendency to be scrutinized and judged more severely.

Before deciding to seek fame and fortune, it is best to consider all of the less desirable possibilities this attention might convey. Few people can withstand having their dirty laundry paraded before the world. We all want privacy. But once we are under the microscope, it is difficult to reclaim an old way of life.

❧

The Leper and Elijah
(Yiddish/Jewish)

The prophet Elijah appeared before God to offer his critique of the way God was running the world. "Look at the way people live," Elijah said. "Can't you see that many people need help?"

"Very well," God said, "Go to earth and have at it. If you can do a better job with people than I have done, you are to be commended."

Now it happened that at one of the Jerusalem gates there sat a leper who begged from those who went in and out of the city. One day the prophet Elijah visited the city and saw the leper at the gate. "I'm an uncle of yours," Elijah told the leper. "And I would like to help you."

So Elijah took the leper, bought him nice clothes and a hat, and got him a job as an apprentice to a baker. Some time later Elijah returned and asked him, "How do you like being a baker?"

"Not very well," the leper replied. "I often burn my hands."

"Well, what would you like to be, then?" he asked.

"Perhaps a tailor."

So Elijah took the leper and set him up as an apprentice to a tailor. Some time later, he returned and asked, "How do you like being a tailor?"

"Not very well," the leper replied. "I keep sticking myself with a needle."

"Well, what would you like to be, then?"

"Perhaps a shoemaker."

Elijah took the leper and set him up as an apprentice to a shoemaker. Some time later, he returned and asked, "How do you like being a shoemaker?"

"Not very well," he replied. "I keep banging my knees and smearing my hands."

"Well, what would you like to be, then?"

"Perhaps a doctor," said the leper.

So Elijah trained him to be a doctor. Some time later he returned and asked, "How do you like being a doctor?"

"Not very well," he replied. "Life is too busy. I am constantly running to the homes of my patients at a moment's notice, and I get little sleep."

"Well, what would you like to be, then?"

The leper replied, "Perhaps a merchant."

So the prophet set him up as a merchant. But he didn't like this either. Neither did the leper like any of the other occupations he tried. The leper was always unhappy. Either the life was too hard, the pay too low, or the job was too messy. There was not a single occupation that appealed to him. Finally, Elijah asked the leper again, "Well, what would you *really* like to be?"

"Perhaps if I were a king," he replied.

And so Elijah made him a king. But some time later the prophet returned and asked, "So tell me . . . how do you like being a king?"

"Not so well," the leper admitted. "Too many worries. I must take care of so many people and the responsibilities are enormous!"

One more time Elijah asked, "Well, what would you like to be, then?"

The leper said, "I think I would like to be God."

"Well," said Elijah, "I must go to heaven and see what God has to say about it." And so he did.

But when the prophet came before God, the Lord of the Universe told him, "Perhaps now, Elijah, you will understand that I know best. Go back and tell the leper to return to his place at the gate."

•   •   •

There is a great truth of creation: that we are all created differently. This is not only true of our physical selves, but also our giftedness, strengths, and shortcomings. Some have gifts of leadership; others gifts of service. Some are designed for creating; others for helping. Still others have gifts of speech; others gifts of listening.

These insights are important for understanding our place in the world and how we can best find a source of happiness and joy. While it may be true that all have the potential for greatness and leadership, not all are happy in doing so. Some roles produce nothing but despair in certain people, while other roles produce energy and drive.

The secret to life's joy is finding one's place in the world.

The Burden by the Side of the Road
(Sufi)

One morning a Sufi was sitting at a fork in the road when a young man approached and asked to be his disciple.

"Very well," the Sufi replied, "I will teach you for one day."

The student watched as one traveler after another came along, each with a different question about life, direction, or God's ways among people. But the Sufi merely sat with his head bowed in prayer, his face pressed between his knees, and he gave no answer to any of the requests.

One by one the people went away, until the Sufi and the student were alone.

Toward evening, a poor man came down the road carrying an enormous burden. This man stopped to ask the contemplative Sufi the way to the nearest town.

At once the Sufi sprang to his feet, took the poor man's burden upon his shoulders, and escorted him some way down the road. Once the poor man had been set in the right direction, the Sufi returned to his place.

The student asked, "So, is this the secret of wisdom? Was that poor man really a saint in disguise?"

The Sufi laughed and said, "Ah, nothing could be further from the truth. Of all the people we have seen today, that poor man was the only one who truly sought the object he claimed to desire."

•   •   •

The foundation of all decisions and achievements begins with desire, as not all requests and demands are girded with a true hunger in the soul. Desire will make up for many deficiencies, even lack of talent. But without desire, there is no fountain from which one can acquire motivation and energy.

Come Together
(African)

There were three scholars who were wise in books, and a fellow who had little more learning than common sense. One day these four men happened to meet on the road. The three scholars said, "What good is all our book learning if we don't apply our knowledge? We've acquired far too much wisdom to be cooped up here in this little village. We should go out and see the world, for with our superior knowledge, we could surely become wealthy and prosperous."

The commoner said, "Perhaps, but be careful. I am afraid you will discover that the world itself is much different than anything you have read in your books."

Scoffing at this bit of advice, the three scholars gathered their things. But before they departed, they invited the commoner to come along with them to see the world. "Come with us," they said, "and we will show you how our learning is superior to any way of the world."

The commoner agreed, and off they went, searching for wealth and fortune. But they had no sooner passed beyond the sight of the town than they came to a dense forest. "Well," said one of the scholars, "we have no choice but to pass through here. That is obvious. A forest is a forest."

"Perhaps so, perhaps not," said the commoner. "It could be a dangerous place."

"Nonsense," said another scholar, and off they went into the forest.

A bit later, the four men came upon the bones of a dead lion. One of the scholars leaned over the remains and said,

"What a wonderful opportunity this is for us to put our great learning to use. I have made a lifelong study of animal skeletons, and I can say with certainty that I know how to reassemble this animal's frame."

The second scholar said, "How splendid. I, too, have a bit of knowledge in this area. I have made a lifelong study of animal tissue. Once you have assembled the bones, I can reattach the sinews and the muscles."

"And as for me," said the third scholar. "I have knowledge of the life forces. If you can erect the skeleton and reattach the muscles and skin, I can make this creature breathe."

The commoner said, "I have no knowledge of these things at all. What can I do but bow before such superior intelligence?"

The scholars went to work. The first assembled the skeleton. The second attached the muscles and flesh. The third began the process of bringing the lion back to life.

But again the commoner spoke up. "My friends, please consider what you are about to do. This animal that you are about to bring to life is a *lion*. If you succeed in this experiment, it will kill us all."

The third scholar said, "Nonsense. What good is superior intelligence unless it can be applied? Now stand back and allow us to demonstrate what we know."

The commoner didn't wait for the culmination of the experiment. Instead, he climbed a tree. He watched from a safe height while the three scholars performed the necessary work on the dead animal. Sure enough, the lion moved.

"A great success!" shouted the first scholar.

"A triumph!" exclaimed the second.

"A testimony to superior learning!" marveled the third.

The lion opened its eyes, moved its tail, and then stood on its feet. When it saw the three men standing nearby, it pounced on them at once and killed them.

The commoner, watching all of this from his safe haven, waited until the lion had gone away. He climbed down from his tree and returned to the village, no wiser perhaps, but alive nonetheless.

•   •   •

Knowledge is not the same as wisdom, and there are many types of intelligence. Common sense may rank as the highest form.

The story reveals a simple truth: just because something is doable does not mean that it should be done. A person might be able to create a device to destroy the world, but for what purpose? Often, it is best to leave some knowledge alone.

The Eyes Have It
(Jewish)

One day Alexander the Great happened to come upon the river of Paradise. As he began to bathe in the water, he found himself transported to heaven. "Open up!" Alexander shouted. "Let me in."

"Only the righteous may enter here," a voice responded.

"Then give me something that I may take back to earth to prove that I have been here," Alexander requested.

Amazingly enough, the gate of heaven opened and out rolled a human eye. Alexander picked it up, put it in a sack, and returned home, wondering how an eye could possibly prove anything. Of course, no one would believe that he had been to heaven, so he called all his wise men together.

"At the gate of heaven, all I was given was this human eye," he told them. "What does it mean?"

A set of scales was set up and one of the wise men said, "Place the eye on one side of the scale and a piece of gold on the other."

Alexander did this and was astounded to find that the eye weighed more. "How is this possible?"

"Now add a handful of silver coins," the wise ones said.

Coins were added to the gold, but the eye still weighed more. The wise men also asked Alexander to place precious stones and other treasures on the scales, but no matter how much was added, the eye outweighed them all.

"Now remove all of the valuables from the scales," the wise men said, "and place there a pinch of common dust."

Alexander did this, and found that the dust now out-weighed the human eye. "I understand now," Alexander said. "As long as we are alive, we desire everything we see. But when we die, there is no longer any desire, and we become more worthless than dust."

•   •   •

This parable, adapted from the Talmud, offers us the possibility of seeing what is truly valuable in life. Possessions and objects may satisfy for a time, but in the end they offer nothing of a lasting or eternal value.

The true treasures of life can be found in the people, rela-tionships, and love we share. Some of life's most prized com-modities are found in the niches of our homes and communities. All we have to do is open our eyes and see.

The Way of Forgetfulness
(Taoist)

Once there lived a hunchback who had a deformed body. However, he was eloquent of speech, and often entertained the prince with his dancing and sleight of hand. The prince liked the hunchback so much that he came to favor other people with skinny necks and plain bodies.

•   •   •

This simple parable concludes with a marvelous observation about life: "When one has an inner strength and character, physical appearance is soon forgotten. When people do not forget what to forget, but forget what not to forget, this is truly forgetting."

When we comprehend this bit of wisdom, we understand that personality is far more important than appearance. Our perceptions of others are merely perceptions. When we learn to look beyond the surface of another person, we begin to under-stand the nature of love.

The Tattooed Sailor
(Sufi)

A sailor went to an artist to have a lion tattooed on his back. He told the artist what he wanted, but as soon as he felt the first sting of the needle, the sailor let out a cry of pain. "Stop immediately," he said. "Whatever you are working on, leave that part out."

"I'm drawing the lion's tail," said the artist.

"Forget the tail," the sailor said. A bit later, he let out another cry of pain. "What are you doing now?" he asked.

"I'm drawing the lion's ear."

"Leave off the ear," the sailor said. "It's too painful." Moments later, he let out another cry. "And now which part are you working on?"

"I'm drawing the lion's stomach," came the reply.

"I'll take the lion without the belly," the sailor said. "Too much pain."

Frustrated by the sailor's requests, the tattoo artist threw down his tools and said, "A lion without a tail, no ears, and no stomach. Who can possibly create such a thing? Even God couldn't do it!"

•   •   •

This parable is typical of Sufi wisdom. An ordinary event is analyzed for its spiritual dimension—with a touch of humor, of course.

In this little tale, impatience is placed under the microscope for a closer inspection. What we discover is this: people are often unprepared to endure the sacrifice and suffering necessary to achieve a desired end. Some quit at the first hint of discomfort. Others give up when they encounter an inconvenience. And some retreat at the first sign of resistance.

However, any worthy goal must be approached with resolve and determination. Pain is a part of life. A person must have strength and tenacity to accomplish a worthwhile goal.

Three Talented Friends
(African)

Three young men went into the fields to harvest grain. When it began to rain, one of the young men filled his basket with grain and placed it on top of his head. On his way home, his foot slipped in the mud and he began to slide. He slid for miles. But as he passed by a house, he reached in through a window, took a knife, and began to cut grass reeds as he slid along. As he continued to slide, he wove a soft mat from the reeds. At last, when he landed, he threw the mat in front of himself to break his fall. As he sat in the mud he said, "See, if I had not had the presence of mind to weave a mat while I was sliding, I would most surely have broken my neck."

The second young man had forty chickens in his basket. On his way home he stopped to let the chickens loose so they could eat. A hawk swooped down to grab one of the chickens, but the young man ran from chicken to chicken, covering each one with the basket. Then he snatched the hawk by its talons and said, "You will have to be quicker than this if you are going to steal one of my chickens."

The third young man had gone hunting with a friend. His friend shot an arrow at an antelope. The young man leaped forward at the same instant, caught the antelope, killed it, skinned it, cut it up, and dried the meat in the sun before putting it inside his knapsack. Then he reached out his hand and caught his friend's arrow. "What are you trying to do?" he asked his friend. "Shoot an arrow through my knapsack?"

• • •

Like many African parables, this tale offers some magical fare seasoned with a bit of humor. The story offers a glimpse into African life and some of the daily activities young men might compete at.

What makes this story so wonderful is the notion that, even when everything goes bad, we can still find a reason to laugh.

The Wisdom of God
(Kashmiri)

One day a dejected fellow sat down under a nut tree to contemplate his difficulties. As he brooded over his lot in life, he noticed a pumpkin vine with several large pumpkins near the base of the tree.

"See," the fellow said to himself, "even God is foolish. Why, if God were clever, He would not only have created a world without misery but would also have used His power more wisely. Consider this nut tree. Here is a strong, vibrant tree capable of producing pumpkins, yet it is filled with tiny nuts that carry no weight at all. And this weak little vine, which looks like it could die at any moment, is supporting several large pumpkins. If God were wiser, those pumpkins would be growing on the tree, and the nuts would be growing on the vine."

As the fellow was pondering the weight of his wisdom, suddenly a nut fell from the tree and landed squarely atop his head. The man looked up, rubbed his chin, and then said, "Oh, God, forgive me. If one of those pumpkins had fallen on my head, I'd be a dead man. Great is your wisdom."

•   •   •

At one time or another, most of us wish we could change the world—or some small piece of it, anyway. We see possibilities for improvement. We desire to make life more just. Or we wish we could change how society acts. But in our haste we can be shortsighted.

Sooner or later we learn to accept the world as it is—in all its strangeness and wonder. That doesn't mean we give up on change, it simply means we come to depend on the world as we experience it. We learn to live with the world as it is, and gather the strength to cope with the problems we must face each day.

All Things Are Possible
(Sufi)

Mulla Nasrudin was attacked by a group of hoodlums who threw rocks at him. Mulla remained calm, however, and began to talk to the boys. "If you stop this attack," he said, "I'll let you in on a little secret."

The attackers put down their rocks and said, "OK, but we want none of your philosophy."

Nasrudin told them, "I have heard that the Sultan is having a big party tonight and everyone is invited." Mulla went on to describe the food, the festivities, and the important guests who would be in attendance. Before he was done with his story, the hoodlums were dancing in their socks, eager to get home and prepare themselves for the party of a lifetime.

Mulla watched as the boys ran away, then smiled at his deception. Suddenly he grew serious and began running toward the Sultan's palace. "It's possible, just possible," he said, "that there really is a party there!"

• • •

A vivid imagination can open a world of possibilities and can take us to places we could only dream about. Imagination, when it becomes vision, can even provoke others to action. It can also allow us to suspend our senses—at least for awhile.

It may also be true that we become what we imagine. People of position usually envision themselves in these roles, and work for them. The clearer our vision of what *could be,* the greater the possibility that it *will be.*

9

Seeking a Guiding Light

The soul can split the sky in two,
And let the face of God shine through.
> —Edna St. Vincent Millay

L ife doesn't come with an instruction manual. But the centuries have revealed others wiser than ourselves who have offered insights and guidance for living. Some of this guidance comes in the form of spiritual advice or teaching, some in the form of practical advice or common sense; other forms may lean heavily toward personal revelation.

Regardless, everyone needs a mentor, or perhaps a therapist, to help guide the way through the labyrinth of this world. With an ever-changing landscape of desires, hopes, and choices, people have a tendency to become overwhelmed by life's demands.

Moments of renewal and recreation are needed to nourish the soul as well as the body. Without opportunities for contemplation and silence, the mind becomes clouded with mere busyness and clutter. Creativity ceases. Productivity falters.

Guidance can come, however, in many forms. A moment of laughter can provide a much-needed glimpse of what is truly important. A well-turned phrase can offer a sudden revelation of a long-forgotten truth. An insightful story might provide just the antidote for a soul weighed down with the cares and burdens of life.

Here are parables of guidance and wisdom from a mix of sources—each basking in its own indelible light. These parables contain hope and joy. Most of all, these tales will provide moments of revelation, sources of light that will not only illuminate the path, but also provide strength for the journey.

How to Become a Buddha
(Zen Buddhist)

A student named Ma-tsu was found in the monastery deep in meditation. His master, seeing Ma-tsu in this posture day after day, approached him with this question: "Why are you sitting in meditation?"

"I wish to become a Buddha," Ma-tsu answered.

Hearing this, the master picked up a piece of tile and began rubbing it vigorously against a stone.

Ma-tsu asked, "What are you doing with the tile?"

"I am polishing this tile to make a mirror," the teacher answered.

"But how can you make a mirror by rubbing a tile?" Ma-tsu asked.

"How can one become a Buddha by sitting in meditation?" asked the master.

•   •   •

Unlike other faiths, Zen Buddhism often mocks the very forms of devotion and practice it espouses. The idea here is that, while meditation is necessary for enlightenment, one should never rely solely on this practice to achieve the end. New ways are necessary. Creativity is needed.

By leaving behind the familiar and the tried-and-true, we can frequently enter new forms of awareness. If the world around us does not change, we can often find a new perspective by changing ourselves, or at least by changing the vantage point from which we observe our situation.

Just as a writer might find new inspiration and insights from a change of venue, so every person can gain a new appreciation of his or her circumstances by taking risks, venturing down new paths, or reaching for new experiences. The greatest enemy of the human spirit is apathy or boredom. We find excitement, however, when we are solving new challenges.

On a spiritual level, this is a reminder that God is always doing a new thing, and those who would be at one with God will find great joy in stretching the imagination toward all that is fresh and beautiful.

The Meaning of Work
(Desert Fathers)

Young John came to the leader of the community and said, "I wish to be free from my labors so I can worship God without distraction." After saying this, he removed his vestments and retreated into the desert.

A week later, however, weary and worn, Young John returned to the community and knocked on the teacher's door. From inside he heard a voice, "Who is it?"

"It is John," he said.

The teacher said, "That cannot be. John is now holy. He has become an angel. He no longer lives in this community."

"But it is me!" John shouted.

The teacher, however, did not open the door until the next morning. When he did answer the door, he told John, "If you are a human being, you must work in order to live."

John answered, "Forgive me, Teacher, for I was wrong."

•   •   •

Is forgiveness possible? Surely it is, when one is able to embrace hospitality and see beyond the past.

But this little parable is also about the nature of worship and study. One who leaves behind community for the purpose of knowing nothing but God may quickly discover that God will not provide everything. People need each other. And most commonly we experience God through human contact and through our capacity to contribute to the common good.

Being spiritual is not so much a quest for the extreme as it is a search for the God who is present in the proximity of others and in daily life. God's presence is everywhere. One can journey a thousand miles to see a flower but miss the bloom growing at one's feet. Likewise, one can find God in holy places without ever leaving home. The true sanctuary of God is the human heart.

How to Have a Good Argument
(Jewish)

Two women were engaged in a bitter argument. Since they were unable to settle their dispute, they asked a wise woman of the community to settle their differences for them. Instead, the wise woman told them a story:

"Once a woman dropped a sack of grain into a deep ravine. She studied the situation for a long time, but could not find a way to retrieve her goods. So she asked some people who were passing along the road, 'How might I retrieve my sack of grain from the ravine?'

" 'Perhaps,' one of them said, 'you could lower a rope and climb down.'

"Another said, 'Perhaps you could buy a donkey and go down into the ravine to retrieve the sack.'

"But the woman replied, 'Oh, my. I don't have a rope and I can't afford a donkey. How will I be able to solve my problem?'

"Then one of the people responded, 'Perhaps it would have been better if you had not dropped the sack of grain into the ravine in the first place.' "

•   •   •

This Talmudic parable is typical of the traditional style of rabbinic teaching common in the first and second centuries. If there was a lesson to be taught, a story was told to illustrate the point.

The guidance found in this story may seem little more than common sense, but as the tale illustrates, we can often avoid difficulty altogether by steering clear of trouble. If friends argue about certain subjects, it is best to avoid those topics. If there are two possible courses of action, it is best to choose the one that will not harm a relationship. Or if trouble is approaching, it can often be avoided by fleeing its path. Sometimes the best results can be found in a life built on stability and carefulness.

Sand Castles
(Buddhist)

Some children were playing on the beach. Each one made sand castles and afterwards said, "This one is mine. Don't touch it." In this manner they defended their sand castles and would not allow any of the other children to stand nearby.

One child, however, came upon another's sand castle in curiosity and kicked it over, destroying it completely. The child who had built the sand castle flew into a rage, began to beat the other child, and called out to the other children, "Look, my castle is destroyed! Help me punish this rule breaker as he deserves!"

The other children followed along and began to beat the child, hitting him with sticks and kicking him until he lay, unmoving, on the ground. Once this was accomplished, all the children returned to making and protecting their own sand castles, telling the others, "Stay away! This is mine! Don't touch my sand castle!"

As evening approached, however, and the darkness began to settle over the beach, each of the children turned from his sand castle, one by one, and thought about going home. The children forgot about their sand castles, or lost interest in them entirely. Some kicked over their castles. Others mashed their castles with their hands. Some abandoned their castles when they lost interest in them.

One by one they returned home, and by the time it was dark, the tide had come in and washed all the castles away.

• • •

This insightful parable, of course, has nothing to do with children, but everything to do with the possessiveness and self-interest that is rampant in the world. Perhaps the metaphor of children is used to show the foolishness of human greed, or to demonstrate the childishness of human behavior.

Regardless, the imagery of the story is penetrating.

A startling truth is that we bring nothing into the world, and we leave with nothing. How we live in the interim is what we call life—and the manner in which we live has a great impact on the world around us. The story holds a promise for those who seek to overcome materialism or elitism.

As the parable reveals, death is the great equalizer—as possessions and individual pride and accomplishments are washed away in the end. But the guidance of the parable may be found in the stark portrait it paints of human life. Everyone must share the same world. Space is precious. But when people forget to care for each other, order breaks down.

Eventually, all things perish. The only enduring gifts are the ones we give to others.

The Pearl
(Gospel of Thomas)

Jesus said, "The kingdom of the Father is like a merchant who received a large supply of goods. As he was sorting through the goods he discovered a pearl. Now, the merchant was wise and crafty. First he sold the goods and then he bought the pearl. You, too, seek the unfailing and enduring treasure."

• • •

Similar to the parable of the pearl found in the New Testament gospels, this story illustrates the meaning of the kingdom of God, according to Jesus. God's work and presence are always nearby, but may be missed by those who look in the wrong places. There is mystery and majesty to God's work that cannot be explained in earthly terms.

Likewise, God's mystery cannot be grasped easily. Like a rare pearl, God is often discovered or known in unexpected ways. All one can do is accept and enjoy the companionship of God, and so enter the kingdom.

Those who are willing to leave behind old ways, step out on faith, and embrace what God is offering are the ones who discover this rare pearl. Sometimes sacrifice is needed. But always there is more to be gained with the help of God.

Heads and Tails
(Buddhist)

There was a bird of the Himalayas that had two heads. One of the heads saw the other head eating some delicious fruit, became jealous, and said to itself, "I shall punish the other head for this breech of etiquette by eating poison."

And so it did . . . and the entire bird died.

Nearby there was a snake whose head and tail constantly quarreled. The tail always wanted to lead, but the head refused.

The tail said, "You are always leading. Every now and then, you should let me be in charge." But the head replied, "Of course I lead. That is the nature of being the head. There is no way I can change places with you. It is a law of nature."

Day after day the quarrel continued. Finally the tail fastened itself to a tree and refused to let go. The head tried to proceed, but the tail refused to budge. When the head tried to pull away, the tail let go, and the entire snake fell into a fire and perished.

•   •   •

Who says that two heads are better than one? In fact, it is extremely difficult to follow more than one leader. Jealousy, bitterness, and rivalry flare when more than one aspires to take up the mantle of leadership.

On a personal level, we must have unity of purpose, of mind, and of will in order to achieve a goal. When our motives are conflicted, or we lost sight of what we are trying to achieve, we rarely succeed. In the same way, we can be very busy without having a clear purpose for our actions. But if we begin with a clear purpose in mind, we are less likely to waste time in trivial work that does not help us to achieve the goal.

The Courageous Fox
(Jewish)

A fox was speaking to the other animals one day and told them the lion had become angry.

"Who will go on our behalf to pacify the lion?" the animals asked.

"Come along with me," the fox said. "I know three hundred parables that will calm him down."

"Let's go," the animals said.

As they began walking toward the lion's den, the fox suddenly stopped in his tracks.

"What's wrong?" the animals wanted to know.

"I forgot a hundred of the parables," the fox answered.

"Surely two hundred will be enough," they said.

The fox walked a bit farther and stopped again.

"Now what's wrong?" the animals asked.

"I just forgot another one hundred parables!"

"Surely a hundred will be sufficient," they said.

A third time the fox stopped and they asked what was wrong. The fox answered, "I forgot the remaining hundred parables! Go on without me, and try to pacify the lion on your own."

•   •   •

Not all who aspire to leadership are capable of leading. Some will falter as a result of their own inadequacies; some will hide behind the strength of others. Chief among these shortcomings is forgetfulness and fear.

As the parable demonstrates, when faced with a great battle, it is not always the most vocal or intelligent who lead the charge. Many would-be leaders shy away from the heat of the conflict. True leadership is never granted by position or education. Leadership is earned through the respect and trust of one's peers.

A good story may sound impressive, but when a community is looking for leadership, it wants courage and conviction. Action is required, not verbal banter.

How to Capture the Wind
(Desert Fathers)

A disciple came to Father Poemen with a concern. "Evil and perverse thoughts keep popping into my head," the disciple confessed.

Father Poemen took the disciple outside and asked him to open his robe and capture the wind.

"Capture the wind?" said the confused disciple. "Surely such a thing is impossible."

"In like manner," Father Poemen answered, "you will be unable to keep such thoughts from popping into your head. All you can do is stand firm against them."

•   •   •

This is a parable of grace. Here is a gentle reminder that indiscriminate thoughts, and focused meditation, are very different in nature. On the one hand, a thought enters the mind—most often arbitrarily. But on the other hand, meditation is the subtle art of rooting out unwanted thoughts, choosing instead those ideas that are noble and beautiful.

In addition, this parable reminds us: we become what we think about.

A Bowl by Any Other Name
(Zen Buddhist)

In the monastery there were two golden bowls from which everyone drank. The master called for two monks and gave them each a bowl to clean.

One monk took his bowl to the river, where he proceeded to scrub it with sand and water. He scraped the bowl until it shone. Still not satisfied, he applied acid and scoured the bowl until it glistened.

The other monk took his bowl and sat quietly in meditation for some time, then, taking a clean towel, he cleaned the bowl in a single swipe.

Each brought his bowl to the master. The first was bright and glistening. But only the second held water.

•　　•　　•

How quickly we can lose sight of our purpose or of what is truly important. Our heads can be turned by the sight of riches and our lives redirected by the promise of fortune. But when we understand why we are here and comprehend the place of all things, we gain enlightenment.

There are also times when we can become fixated on minor details and completely miss the purpose of an activity or event. It's the age-old difference between living to work, or working to live. In life it is important to focus on the major goals. If we don't, we can often become lost in the minor details.

The Most Valuable Thing in the World
(Sufi)

A humble dervish came before the king with a question: "If you were dying of thirst in the desert, what would you give for a cup of water?"

The king answered, "I would give half my kingdom."

The dervish continued, "Then suppose after you drank, your stomach became bloated and you were on the verge of death. What would you give for the medicine tablets that would make you whole?"

The king responded, "Why, the other half of my kingdom, without doubt."

"Why is it, then," the dervish asked, "that you place such enormous value on your kingdom when, by your own admission, it is worth only a cup of water and a few medicine tablets?"

• • •

We can often gain a new appreciation of our values by placing ourselves in hypothetical situations. In a life-threatening situation, what would be kept? What would be forfeited? Such questions can help us to gauge what is truly important.

Basic necessities such as food and water take on high priority when we are thirsty or hungry. A lifeboat on a sinking ship is of greater value than a pocketful of gold.

The parable might also help us to appreciate the blessings we have received. After all, taking life for granted shortchanges our sense of life's possibilities. We live a fuller life when we are mindful of the gifts we receive each day.

The Riddle of the Strongest
(Based on a story from 1 Esdras)

King Darius of Persia had a great banquet, and afterward there were three young men who aspired to become counselors to the throne. They came together and proposed a contest before the king. "We will offer answers to a riddle," they said. "The question shall be: 'What is the most powerful thing in the world?'" The king agreed, and each set about trying to formulate the wisest response.

The first man offered his answer. "Isn't it obvious that wine is the strongest?" he asked. "Consider these facts. Wine betrays the thoughts of all who drink it, so that the thoughts of a king are equal to the thoughts of an orphan. The mind of the slave is made equal to the mind of the free, and the rich mind is made equal to the mind of the poor. Wine turns even the saddest moments into times of feasting and joy, and those who drink it forget who is friend or enemy, family or foe. Moreover, when one recovers from the wine, there is no memory of what one has said or done. I ask you: is not wine the most powerful thing in the world?"

The king and the other two men considered this answer, but right away the second man spoke up. "Wine is indeed a good answer. But, I ask you, isn't a king more powerful than wine? Consider this: a king is lord and master of everything. He rules over land, sea, and all the people who inhabit the earth. When a king sends soldiers to war, they go to war. When he tells them to attack, they attack. If he tells them to go over that wall, or destroy that tower, or overtake that city, they do it, even though many will be killed.

"When the war is over, the soldiers bring all of the spoils back to the king. And the king, what does he do? He sits, reclines, eats and drinks, and does whatever he pleases whenever he wants. Others wait to do his bidding, and no one is able to turn aside from a request made by the king. Doesn't this show that a king is by far the most powerful in the world?"

Again, the other two men and the king considered this answer. But before anyone could speak, the third man spoke up. "Yes, these are both good answers. Wine is strong. And the king is great and powerful. But, I ask you, are not women stronger? Consider these facts. Only women can have children. Women gave birth to everyone who walks the earth—even the king. And women gave birth to those who plant vineyards and press wine. Women also care for men, and bring them glory.

"If a man obtains any silver or gold, what does he do with it? He gives it to a woman. This proves that a man would rather have the beauty of a woman near him than the beauty of silver or gold. Also, when a man crosses the ocean or the desert in search of riches, or if he goes off to war, he spends all his time dreaming about a woman, hoping one day to return to her. And when a man grows old, he longs to live out his days with the woman who has been at his side.

"Likewise, consider all the dangers a man will face for a woman. He will sail the high seas, tangle with lions, take up the sword, or walk through darkness and deprivation—all for the sake of the woman he loves. Why, some men have even lost their minds because of women, and others have become slaves because of them.

"Why, even the king is not immune to the power of women. I have seen it myself. When a woman from the king's harem comes into the room and smiles at him, he goes all to pieces. He will laugh, blush, or stare at her with his mouth open. So, even though wine is strong, and the king is stronger than wine, women are more powerful than them both!"

When the king and the other two men heard this answer, they were impressed, but just as the king was about to speak, the third fellow continued even further with his answer.

"But wait," he said. "I am not through. There is another thing that is more powerful than these other three!"

"And what is that?" asked the king.

"It is truth," the fellow answered. "Truth will endure and prevail forever. But as for wine, it will go bad. The king will perish. And women will die, too. Truth never passes away.

"When someone offers an insight under the influence of wine, truth will reveal whether the statement will endure. And when the king issues a decree, truth will determine whether the king's edict will stand the test of time. And as for people—only truth will tell whether their lives were based on good or bad deeds. For all of these reasons and more, truth is the most powerful thing in the world."

When the king heard this answer, he was moved—as were the other two men. And so the king rewarded this fellow with honor and great riches.

• • •

Is there anything that will endure forever? Who knows? But we know that truth survives.

In a world where there are many passing voices and fleeting enticements, it is rare to find discussion of enduring issues. We are often so busy, we don't have time to discuss the issues that matter. The parable offers an opportunity to pause and consider the truths we have learned, and to appreciate those gifts that will one day pass away.

What the Caged Bird Knows
(Jewish)

There was a beautiful bird that was confined to a cage. One day another bird flew up and perched nearby. It told the beautiful bird, "How fortunate you are to have a servant who brings you food and water daily."

The caged bird answered, "Ah, but you see only the benefits. When you are on the outside looking in, it is difficult to see the bars."

• • •

Perspective does matter. How we see an object or a situation is greatly influenced by our attitude and vantage point. A glance, an action, a word—all of these can be interpreted or misinterpreted in a variety of ways, and each can lead to reconciliation or war, peace or anger.

It may also be true that we can choose to see what we want to see in life. We can look for beauty or misery. We can see wonder and awe in a particular day, or drudgery and boredom.

The parable is reminiscent of the adage:

> Two looked out from the prison bars,
> One saw mud, the other stars.

Lord Krishna's Request
(Hindu)

Lord Krishna summoned two kings in order to test their wisdom. To the first king he offered this challenge: "Travel throughout the world, search high and low, and see if you can find a truly good person."

The first king roamed the earth, talked to many people, and some time later returned to Krishna with his report. "I have done as you requested," the king said. "I traveled the earth, but was unable to find a single good person from among so many. All people are corrupt. Not a single one has a good heart."

Krishna then called for the second king. To him he offered this challenge: "Travel throughout the world, search high and low, and see if you can find a truly wicked person."

This king departed, talked to many people, and some time later returned to Krishna. "I have done as you requested," the king said. "I traveled the earth, but was unable to find a truly wicked person. Many are misguided, many walk in darkness, some are full of failure, but as for a truly wicked person, there is not one to be found."

• • •

The parable needs little explanation. Humanity is a mixed bag—as is each person. All have strengths and weaknesses, successes and failures, blessings and sins. Learning to see the best in others is a mark of wisdom.

The parable also encompasses the affirmation that something of the divine exists in all people. If all are created in God's image, then surely there is some good to be found in everyone. There may also be failure and wickedness, but the highest principle prevails.

We are changed when we look for the good in others.

The Meaning of Progress
(Taoist)

Yen Hui told Confucius, "I have made progress."

Confucius said, "Tell me about this."

Yen Hui said, "I no longer worry about people and have no responsibility."

Confucius answered, "This is good, but not enough."

Some days later, Yen Hui approached Confucius again and said, "I have made progress."

Confucius said, "Tell me what you mean."

Yen Hui answered, "I no longer give any thought to ritual or music."

"This is good, but not enough," said Confucius.

Later, Yen Hui approached Confucius and said, "I have made progress."

Confucius said, "Tell me about it."

Yen Hui answered, "I sit in forgetfulness."

Confucius was surprised and said, "Tell me what you mean by 'sitting in forgetfulness.'"

Yen Hui said, "I give no mind to my body and do not rely on my intellect; I have forgotten about my self, have forsaken understanding, and have become one with the Universe."

When Confucius heard this, he said, "When everything is the same, there are no preferences; when everything is changing, there is no constant. Can it be that you have obtained such wisdom? If so, I would follow you."

·   ·   ·

In Taoism, one encounters the concept of *wei wu wei*, which means roughly "doing not doing." The idea has nothing to do with passivity, but, rather, practicing righteous living and awareness to the point where one's actions flow from the center of being. Much as an athlete might master certain movements to the point where she becomes unaware of these movements, or a painter might master the stroke of a brush without having to think about it—so it is with *wei wu wei*. In Taoism, one becomes as one with the universe when he or she masters "doing not doing."

This parable provides a glimpse of the type of understanding one is expected to attain when one reaches this state of wisdom. Those who learn to let go of the self can become more proficient. Those who release desire and attachment are free to live in love and harmony. The goal of Taoism is to become Tao, the Truth, the Life.

10

The Strength of a
Virtuous Life

Assume a virtue, if you have it not.
—William Shakespeare

C onfucius once said, "Virtue does not live alone; she must have neighbors." This definition, in essence, is what a virtuous life is about. Goodness, honesty, fidelity, patience, love—these and other virtues have little meaning outside of their connection in human relationships. In fact, it would seem odd to refer to someone as virtuous who does not exhibit such attributes in his dealings with others. A virtuous life is defined by the quality of one's relationships and interpersonal decisions.

Through the centuries, many have taught the virtuous life through precept and example. All religious traditions lift up favorite sons and daughters to serve as guides to a higher life. Some were visible martyrs. Others lived out the fullness of their lives in humility and relative obscurity.

There were also teachers who took another path. Confucius taught the precepts of the virtuous life through simple observation and highlighted examples from daily life and service. Jesus offered a path of love, even toward one's enemies, and taught the virtue of radical sacrifice to God. Jewish mystics offered devotion to the highest laws of God and neighbor. Islamic poets used humor and imagery to subdue the heart and turn attention to God's benevolence.

The virtuous life, however, need not be attached to a religious tradition to be valid. Nearly all cultures and peoples share common expectations and mores that point to the useful life. Examples of kindness, generosity, and humility can be found everywhere. Parables of integrity, patience, and gratitude may be mined from any land.

Here one can find fresh perspectives that might open a window to a new and better life. Perhaps new insights may be gained. Change can occur.

No one lives a virtuous life free of struggle, self-doubt, or imperfection. That is part of the incompleteness of the human experience. There is always a need to grow, to become tomorrow what we are not today. But without courage and persistence, nothing is possible.

All of the parables in this chapter have something to offer the dreamer or the seeker. Some teach love and encouragement; others teach through their ability to present old ideas in new ways; still others use negative effect to produce a positive result. Most of all, the stories are stepping-stones through which we may embrace goodness, compassion, or mercy. One story at a time, one day at a time, we face the difficulties and challenges and learn to how to live a virtuous life.

The Great Way
(Confucian)

There was the time Confucius was taking part in a winter sacrifice. But after it was over, he took a walk along the top of the wall, sat down, and sighed sorrowfully as he looked out over the city of Lu.

His disciple asked, "Why the sorrowful sigh?"

Confucius answered him, "Those who once practiced the Great Way during the time of the Three Dynasties, I will never get to meet. But when the Great Way was practiced, everyone shared all things. Those who were worthy and able did not just help themselves, but practiced generosity and affection for each other. They did not regard only their parents as their parents, only their children as their children, but the widow, the orphan, and the lonely were all embraced and cared for. The energies of the people were used for the good of all, and by this outlook evil was prevented, thieves and revolutionaries did not exist, and people could leave their houses unlocked. This was the age of the Grand Unity.

"Now the Great Way is no more, and interests have become a private matter. Only one's parents are regarded as one's parents, only one's children are regarded as one's children, and all labor is for selfish ends."

• • •

Every person, as he or she gets older, has a tendency to see the past through rose-colored lenses. When we were young, of course, the world was a better place, people behaved differently, and there was less evil and confusion in the world. As we get older, we tend to see the world as a mess. We like to think that life was better way back when.

As with every age and time, the past always seems so much more complete, so perfect, and so sublime. But is this true?

In one sense, yes. The past is a more complete and less confusing time because we have already lived it. There is a tendency to remember the good and to forget the bad. Nostalgia and selective memory kick in. But on another level, the past is no more promising than the future. As with any time or place or people, all of life changes, and we are forced to change with it. In essence, the future is what we make of it.

Confucius knew this. We sigh for what we have left behind— some part of ourselves that we cannot reclaim, years already lived, opportunities lost. But we also sigh for the days ahead, days we must face with courage and conviction.

At its deepest level, this parable hints at the challenges each person must embrace, and the changes needed in individual and social life if people are to reclaim what they believe has been lost.

Simplicity of Virtue
(Taoist)

Lao Tzu once told Confucius, "Have you observed that chaff from the winnowing will blind a man's eyes so that he cannot see a compass? Do you not know that mosquitoes will keep a man awake all night? In the same way, constant talk of charity and duty drives me mad. Strive to recover the simplicity of the world. Just as the wind blows where it wants to go, so let virtue establish itself without forcing it."

•   •   •

Strive as we might, we can never force another person to live according to our values, beliefs, or code of ethics. Every person must discover the highest path for himself. Forcing codes of conduct may even produce the opposite effect.

The parable reflects two approaches to the age-old question: Is it possible to force values upon others? Confucius seemed to think so. But Lao Tzu took the opposite position, believing that constant talk of virtues and values did little to change society. He advocated striving for simplicity, meaning those of high virtue would be as leaven in the loaf.

As with many Taoist parables, here are two sides to the same coin—the yin and yang. Both positions may have validity. But what is needed most is a balance between the two.

On Kindness to Animals
(Islamic)

Muhammad observed: "An adulteress was passing by a well when she saw a dog, its tongue hanging out with thirst. The woman took off her boot, tied it to a rope, let it down, and gave the animal a drink. She polluted the water, but was forgiven for the act.

"Are there rewards for doing good to animals, being kind to beasts of burden, and giving them drink? Indeed, there are heavenly rewards for such kindness to animals."

•   •   •

This is a story from the Hadith—the oral traditions attributed to the prophet Muhammad. Among these traditions are stories that address a variety of topics and issues. Here, a question about kindness to animals is addressed.

Long before the days of animal rights or activist organizations, this parable offers a simple answer to the questions surrounding the ethical treatment of animals. If an animal is in need, we should try to meet that need. No animal should have to suffer without reason.

If kindness is a virtue, then it should extend to all creatures. Respect is due all living things.

A Drink of Water
(Buddhist)

The Buddha was passing through a village one day and came upon a well. A young woman was there and the Buddha asked her for a drink of water. When she saw who was speaking to her, she said, "I am unworthy to give you a drink of water. I am of the lowest caste, and would only pass along my impurity."

The Buddha replied, "But I did not ask you for your caste. I asked you for a drink of water."

•   •   •

What is compassion? Surely it has to do with breaking down barriers and walls that divide people—barriers between the rich and the poor, the sick and the healthy, the devout and the searching. The greatest compassion is shown when one can lay aside one's own rules and values and enter the life of another person.

As this parable demonstrates, we are all needy at heart. Compassion is necessary in every avenue of life.

Although this is a parable of the Buddha, it is mildly reminiscent of the story of Jesus and the woman at the well of Samaria—another story of compassion—found in the New Testament.

The Contest
(Chinese)

A man from Ch'u was in charge of the sacrifices offered to the gods. He gave his assistants a goblet of wine to share.

The assistants said, "There is not enough for all of us. Let us have a contest. We shall each draw a snake in the dirt, and the one who finishes first will get the wine."

They agreed and began to draw in the sand. The one who finished first reached out his hand and took the goblet. He held it to his lips with one hand while his other hand continued to draw. "See," he said to the others, "I can even make feet on my snake."

But before he could drink, another man finished his snake, grabbed the goblet of wine and said, "There is no such thing as a snake with feet." And he drank the wine immediately.

•   •   •

This parable, from the writings of the classical teacher Chan Kuo-ts'e, reveals several virtues for our consideration. First, we should always be humble in the face of imminent victory. Premature celebration or disrespect for our opponents can often lead to defeat.

Persistence is also a virtue. The end of the race is what matters—not the beginning. Those who stay the course often gain the crown in the end.

The parable also reveals the importance of honor, especially with regard to our peers. A level playing field is most important if we are to gain a true understanding of another person's strengths and challenges.

Finally, should we be victorious in competition, there is nothing wrong with a bit of celebration. We should reward ourselves when we have achieved something important. Celebrating our achievements is a wonderful way to build self-esteem and honor the spirit of fair competition.

Service
(Sufi)

One afternoon the wise Sufi said to his disciples, "There are jewels everywhere. Why are you not collecting them?"

The disciples began to search, but no one found a single gem. "We don't see any jewels," they said.

The Sufi answered, "Serve! Serve! That is what I mean!"

•   •   •

Sage advice from an old sage—this parable speaks with simple elegance. In most faiths, service toward one's neighbors is closely linked to devotion to God. If we desire to grow close to God, service is required.

The virtue of sacrifice is one that many aspire to, but it is most difficult to achieve.

The Beauty of Kindness
(Traditional Japanese)

There once lived a kind old man and woman who were very poor. In the winter, the old man sold kindling in the village, and would often trudge through the snow in order to make enough money to buy food.

One day the old man was on his way to the village when he saw something moving alongside the road. Drawing nearer, he discovered a beautiful white crane that had been caught in a trap. Taking pity on the bird, the old man released it from the trap, and it flew off, beating its wings higher and higher into the snowy sky.

When the old man returned home that evening with his meager earnings, his wife was glad to see him. They sat down to eat a small meal together when suddenly there was a knock at the door. "Who could it be this time of night?" wondered the old woman. She went to the door and saw a young girl standing outside, shivering in the cold.

"Please come in," offered the old woman. "Come stand by the fire and tell us what brings you out on a night like this."

"I'm on my way to the village," the girl explained, "but it's too dark and cold to travel. May I stay here for the night?"

Naturally, the old man and woman offered their hospitality. "We are poor people," the old woman explained, "but you are welcome to anything we have."

Now, as it happened, the old man and woman were quite taken with this beautiful girl. Since they had no children of their own, they were impressed by the respect she gave to her elders. When morning came they discovered the snow was still too high for travel, and so they asked the girl to stay with them.

This went on for several days, and the old man and woman both remarked at how much joy and happiness the young girl had brought into their home. They were surprised when, on the sixth morning, the girl asked the old couple for a favor.

"What is it?" asked the old woman. "We have come to love you as our own daughter and will do anything you ask."

The girl bowed to the ground and then said, "My mother and father died recently. I was on the way to the village to live with some relatives whom I hardly know. But I would rather stay here with you. Would that be possible?"

The old couple quickly agreed, but reminded the girl that they had no money. "Don't worry," the girl said. "If you let me stay with you, good things will happen." From that moment on the old couple embraced the girl as their own daughter.

Some days later, the girl set up a wooden loom in a corner of the little house. She put a screen in front of the loom for privacy and asked the old man to buy her some thread the next time he made money in the village. He was glad to help, and when he returned with several spools of beautiful thread, the young girl said, "I am going to weave at the loom, but there is something I need to ask. No matter what happens, neither of you can ever look behind this screen while I am weaving at the loom. Will you promise not to look?"

Again, the old couple agreed.

The next day, the girl worked at the loom all day. The old man and woman kept their promise and did not look behind the screen. Later, the girl brought out a beautiful brocade cloth. It was filled with color and featured two white birds flying against the background of a golden sun. The old couple was moved by its loveliness.

"Take it to the village tomorrow," the girl said. "Please sell it and buy more thread, then I shall make something even lovelier."

Reluctantly, the old man agreed to this, for he felt that it was too beautiful to sell. But the promise of another brocade led him to the village.

That day, a crowd of people gathered around the cloth. There were many who wanted to buy the piece, but the old man waited until a wealthy lord rode by. When the lord saw the beautiful brocade, he offered the old man a bag of gold. Immediately, the old man sold the piece, bought more thread for the young girl, and returned home.

The next day, the girl created another lovely brocade. Again the wealthy lord bought it for a sack of gold.

This exchange continued for several days.

One morning, while the young girl was working at the loom behind the screen, the old woman became curious. "I must have a peek to see how she makes such beautiful cloth," she told her husband.

"No!" he said firmly. "We made a promise. We must keep it."

However, as the days wore on, the old woman's curiosity got the best of her. One afternoon, she slipped over to the screen and peeked at the young girl. But there was no girl behind the screen at all! Instead, she saw a giant white crane sitting at the loom. It was plucking its own feathers and weaving them into beautiful brocades with its beak. Most of its feathers had already been plucked, and it was quite bald.

The old woman let out a scream and ran to the old man with the news. They said nothing to each other the rest of the day, but waited until the young girl was finished at the loom.

At last the young girl stepped out from behind the screen, this time carrying the most beautiful brocade of all. "Thank you for being so kind to me," she said. "But I must go now."

Looking at the old man she said, "I am the crane you freed from the trap. I wanted to repay you for saving my life, but now you know my disguise. However, I leave knowing that you will never be hungry again."

That night, the young girl stepped outside, and at once turned into the beautiful white crane. Higher and higher it flew into the night sky. It circled above the old man and woman three times, and then became as one with the stars.

• • •

There is beauty in kindness, and a good deed rarely goes unrewarded. In Japanese culture, majestic birds are often revered as harbingers of goodness, and one is wise to treat such creatures with respect. After all, one never knows what good fortune may be conveyed through a kind act.

The story serves as a reminder that our attitude makes a difference in how we see life and others. Some see beauty. Others see ugliness. Some people withhold love. Other people give it away. But those who find joy in caring for others are most blessed.

This classic story is one of the most famous folk tales of Japan and is retold in various renditions. In some forms of the story, the beautiful white crane dies at the end—but I chose the happier ending to show that goodness eventually triumphs.

A Time of Power
(Taoist)

In the ancient times, King Yao told his successor, Shun, that he was going to mount an offensive against three neighboring nations, but he also admitted that he was uncomfortable in the position of being ruler. Shun studied the meaning of this and replied, "The kings who rule those nations are as wild animals. Why do you feel uncomfortable? Long ago there were ten suns that appeared and illuminated all the earth. Likewise is not virtue superior to any sun?"

•   •   •

What is power? This parable suggests that true authority rests in virtue rather than position. We need not fear an opposing force when we are in the right. Wrong may prevail for a season but will not endure.

Those who would assume the mantle of leadership are often forced into difficult positions. Sometimes lives are at stake. Sometimes doubts arise. It is truly a lonely existence when one is given ultimate authority.

The best we can do in a position of leadership is to remain true to our values. The principles that have guided people in ages past may be the same principles we can use to make decisions in our times of crisis or indecision.

The Silver Window
(Jewish)

There once lived a man who built a house overlooking a village. Now this man was compassionate and generous, and he always helped his neighbors whenever he could.

As was his habit, he would stand at a large window each morning and look down on the village, count his blessings, and say a prayer for his friends. Each day he would do at least one good deed, and would return to his home joyous and content.

Now it came to pass that the man gained a sizable sum of money. He thanked God for this good fortune and resolved to help others with his money. He did, however, make one concession for himself. He decided to adorn the edges of his favorite window with pure silver.

As the days went by, the man gave to his neighbors. He began every morning by standing at the window giving thanks for his blessings. But he also wondered how much more beautiful the window might be if it had additional silver around the edges.

Days went by, then weeks, then months. As time passed, the fellow gave less of his time and money to those in need and spent more of his wealth on adorning the window. Eventually the entire glass was covered with glowing silver.

In the end, the fellow could no longer see his neighbors from the window. He could only see his own reflection.

•   •   •

Despite our best intentions, wealth can change us. Moreover, wealth has a way of refocusing our priorities and intentions, claiming a bigger share of our souls and weaning us away from deeper relationships with others. Community breaks down when money can satisfy so many of our basic needs.

The parable points to the virtue of service and the need to live in community with others. There is a need for more windows in the world, not more mirrors.

Feeding Chickens
(Jewish)

There was once a very pious fellow who spent all of his time studying the scriptures, praying, and offering invocations to God. He was so pious, in fact, that he rarely had time for anything but God—not even eating or sleeping. Because of his devotion, the fellow found himself becoming poorer and poorer. With all his time spent in prayer, it was difficult to earn a living, and his wife was becoming agitated.

Eventually the poor fellow decided he would seek the wisdom of a noted rabbi. The rabbi listened to the man's story and then asked, "Tell me, what is the first thing you do in the morning?"

"Why, I wash and purify myself for the morning prayers," the fellow answered. "I prepare my clothing, so as to be certain I am doing right before God."

"And what else do you do?" the rabbi wanted to know.

The fellow went on to describe how he devoted himself to God, making certain to complete his morning prayers. In the afternoon, he would finally get around to doing his chores and taking care of business matters.

After listening to his daily rituals, the rabbi offered only one bit of advice: "Feed your chickens."

The fellow went home and at once began to ponder the meaning of the phrase, "Feed your chickens." He was certain that the words had some mystical meaning or contained some bit of metaphorical insight. In fact, he became so infatuated with discovering the mystical meaning of the words, that he devoted even less time to his business. He grew poorer still.

Again he returned to the rabbi. "I am still struggling," he told his teacher. "Tell me what to do if I am to prosper."

"Feed your chickens," was all the rabbi said.

On his way home, the fellow suddenly had a revelation. The rabbi meant exactly what he said. He was to feed his chickens—the chickens in his barnyard, the ones he sold for profit in town.

The next morning, before washing or saying his prayers, the fellow fed his chickens. From that time on, he never wanted again.

•   •   •

Life is made up of priorities. But often we lose sight of what is most important. Sometimes, in our zeal to do the right thing, we can lose sight of the promises we have made. A balanced life is most difficult to create, but is vitally important to our emotional and relational health.

Learning to honor the first things, and to be attentive to them, is one of the greatest signs of maturity. Many needs compete for our attention and time. Learning how to prioritize is crucial.

The truly great men and women of any age are those who understand what needs to be done at any given moment, then do it. Every day there is something important for each of us to accomplish. We are most alive when we stick to our priorities and accomplish, each day, what we have set out to do.

The Donkey's Disguise
(Indian)

There was a fellow who owned a donkey and worked the animal very hard. In time, however, the donkey became worn out. To help the animal recuperate, the owner placed a panther skin on the donkey's back and allowed it to graze in a neighbor's field so people would leave it alone.

Sure enough, when people saw the donkey with the panther hide on its back, they mistook it for a big cat and kept a safe distance.

In time, however, the owner of the field happened to walk by. He was wearing a gray coat, and when he saw the big panther eating grass in his field, he ran the other way. The donkey looked up about this time and happened to mistake the owner for another donkey. It was lonely, so it gave chase.

Naturally, this made the land owner run even faster, but when he heard the panther bray, he knew it was only a donkey covered in a panther skin. The land owner took out a bow and arrow and shot the donkey dead on the spot.

•   •   •

This tale is about character. We can never hide our true selves behind masks, coverings, or outward appearances. Our character is revealed in our words, actions, and attitudes. This parable is reminiscent of the old motto: Be yourself.

A Refusal of Sweetness
(Baha'i)

After the Bab was imprisoned, one of his disciples brought him a jar of honey to sweeten his days in captivity. The Bab took one look at the honey and knew that it was of inferior quality.

He asked the disciple how much he had paid for it and where he had obtained it.

The disciple revealed the price and his source, and the Bab then asked the disciple to take the honey back. When the disciple hesitated, the Bab again asked him to return the honey to the seller. He then explained to the disciple that, by returning the honey, he was giving the seller an opportunity to see the error of his ways and to make things right.

•　　•　　•

In the mid-1800s, the rulers of Persia massacred tens of thousands of people who were part of a new communal sect. These people were followers of a man who later declared himself to be the Bab, "the gate." Although most of the disciples of this community were destroyed, a smaller number founded the Baha'i faith—a religion centered on issues of justice and oppression for the world's peoples. Although the Bab was later executed, his followers did not retaliate or seek vengeance—a testament to peace of the highest order.

This story is a traditional Baha'i tale and offers a bit of sweetness of its own. It is one thing to seek personal honesty, but quite another to offer such an opportunity to one who has fallen. We might call this virtue patience, but it may be more appropriately seen as humility. When we refuse a sweet gift in order to teach another person, this is true goodness.

11

The Gentle Art
of Encouragement

If God be for us, who can be against us?
—Romans 8:31

Few people go through life without experiencing periodic bouts of discouragement. Some of these moments come upon us unexpectedly and may even take hold of us when life is good, while other periods of discouragement hold us hostage in negativity and self-doubt.

Everyone needs a lift now and then. We need bright and beautiful moments to remind us that life holds promise. We need the support of other people—especially in times of difficulty. And we need vision and work to do if we are to embrace the future with confidence and determination.

There is a classic Hassidic story about a young boy who was playing a game of hide-and-seek with some friends. After the boy hid, his friends stopped playing the game and never came to look for him. Disappointed at the outcome of the game, the boy came crying to his grandfather, who embraced him and attempted to soothe his tears with a bit of wisdom.

"There are lessons to learn from our disappointments," the grandfather said. "All of life is like a game between us and God. Only God is the one who is weeping, because we have stopped playing the game. God is waiting to be found. All we have to do is look. Discouragement comes when we go looking for other things."

Like a good friend, a perceptive parable has a way of comforting and guiding at the same time. A story can provide just the antidote for a downcast spirit or help to turn a frown into a smile.

All of the parables in this section will lend encouragement and hope. Some offer a more beautiful vision of what could be. Others provide context for solving problems. A few offer laughter as a cure-all.

There is an African proverb that says: A stone sitting in water cannot comprehend how parched the hill is. Drink deep from these waters if your spirit is parched. Let the encouraging water fill you with new life and energy.

The Return of the Prodigal Son
(A parable of Jesus)

There was a father who had two sons. One day the younger son came to his father and said, "Give me my share of the inheritance now." And so the father divided everything he owned and gave the younger son his half.

Not long after this, the younger son gathered his fortune and departed. He went into a faraway country and squandered everything on his whims and passions. Soon afterward, a severe famine swept over the land and the young man was in desperate need. He became so hungry that he was forced to hire himself out to a local farmer, who put him to work feeding the swine.

While the young man was working among the pigs, he was sometimes so hungry that he even considered eating the slop he was feeding to the hogs. He had nothing.

But when he came to his senses, he said to himself, "What am I doing here? Back home, all of my father's hired hands have enough to eat. And here I am, dying of hunger. I know what I'll do: I'll go home and ask my father's forgiveness.

I will say, 'Father, I am not worthy to be called your son, but I will gladly work as one of your servants.'" So he set out for home.

Now while he was still a long way off, his father saw his son coming up the road and was overcome with compassion. The father ran to meet his son, threw his arms around him, and kissed him.

But the son said, "Father, I have sinned against you and heaven. I am no longer worthy to be called your son."

The father said to his servants, "Quickly! Fetch the finest robe in the house and put it on my son. Put a ring on his finger and sandals on his feet. Get the fatted calf and kill it. Prepare a feast. For my son was dead, and now he lives again. He was lost, but now he has been found."

At that word, everyone in the house began to celebrate.

Now it happened that the elder son was in the fields when his younger brother came home. When the elder son returned from his labors, he heard the sound of a celebration at the house. He asked one of the servants about this.

"Haven't you heard?" the servant said. "Your younger brother has returned. Your father has killed the fatted calf, showered him with presents, and now has prepared a celebration in his honor."

When the older brother heard this, he was furious. He went home, but refused to participate in the celebration. His father came out, pleading for him to come inside and join the party.

But the older brother said, "All of my life I have been faithful to you. I have served you and did whatever you asked. Yet when did you ever give me even a goat with which to celebrate with my friends? Now, this son of yours comes home after wasting his inheritance on gambling and prostitutes, and you kill the fatted calf and have a party!"

The father explained, "My son, you are always here with me. Everything I own is yours. But we had to celebrate and rejoice because this brother of yours was dead, and now lives again. He was lost, and now he has been found."

• • •

Among the many parables attributed to Jesus, the story of the wayward son and the forgiving father ranks as the single greatest for its passion, grace, and vision. Entire books have been written about this parable, and it has inspired the work of artists and poets.

There are many elements to this parable that have universal appeal. The story, for example, demonstrates both the waywardness of human desire (the younger son) and the incomprehensible grace and forgiveness of God (the father). The older son epitomizes established religious communities, an unforgiving spirit, or any proper and right practices that erect walls instead of doorways. God desires reconciliation, not more rules and regulations that keep people apart and prohibit people from experiencing divine grace.

The parable is encouraging because it offers hope for anyone who may be in the far country—that place in life or in our experience where we have turned inward, where we have lost our way, our vision, or our faith in God's love. With God's help, no situation is hopeless.

The story reminds us that there is an underlying grace and mercy to life that we cannot name. This grace carries us in times of need, and sustains us in times of doubt. When we realize this truth, there is always the atmosphere of celebration. Life becomes a party—which is the most intriguing image we have of the world to come.

Spitting on the Rabbi
(Jewish)

On Friday evenings, the rabbi preached powerful sermons in the synagogue. Every week, a certain woman came to listen. She was so moved by his words that she often stayed in the synagogue to pray long after the sermon was over. Her habit, however, was creating a rift between her and her husband.

On Friday evenings the husband would ask, "Where have you been? It's late, and the sermon was over long ago."

The wife would say, "I've been at the synagogue, meditating on the rabbi's words."

This went on for several weeks, until one day the husband demanded that his wife spit in the rabbi's face. When the wife was unwilling to do this, the husband left home in anger. The woman went to her two closest friends and shared her dilemma. They, in turn, went to visit the rabbi.

Two days later, the rabbi called the wife and her two friends into his office and said, "I have a problem to share with you. My eyes have gone bad. I have asked you here today to pray for my healing."

After the women began to pray, the rabbi turned to the wife and said, "It has also been revealed to me that healing may come if a righteous woman spits seven times in my eyes." Moved with pity, the woman came closer to the rabbi and spit seven times in his eyes.

When this was done, the rabbi opened his eyes and smiled. "Go home," he said, "and tell your husband that not only have you spit in the rabbi's face, you have spit upon him seven times."

When others in the synagogue heard what had been done, they were indignant. "You have brought dishonor to your position," they said. "How could you bring such shame to the office of rabbi?"

But the rabbi answered, "My reputation and name are of no value compared to a marriage. This was a small price to pay for peace between a husband and wife."

•   •   •

The best friends are those who can give us what we need without our having to ask for it. They are able to see the awkwardness of a situation and work behind the scenes toward an encouraging outcome.

Pride can get in the way of this endeavor, as can our own shortcomings. But there are times when we need to accept the grace offered by others. We cannot solve every problem on our own. Those who are able to accept the goodwill of others discover an indescribable joy.

God Is Good

(Jewish)

Two men set out on a journey together. One was a believer; the other, a skeptic. They took with them a donkey, a lantern, and a rooster (which always sat on top of the donkey's head).

As they traveled, the believer constantly expressed his faith in God. "God is good in all circumstances," he said.

The skeptic, however, would respond, "Let's wait and see just how good God is."

When they came to the first town, they were disappointed to find that all the inns were filled. Settling in for the night exposed to the elements, the skeptic asked sarcastically, "Well, do you still think God is good?"

"Of course," said the believer. "God has determined that this is the best place for us to sleep tonight."

"But why?" wondered the skeptic.

"It shall be made known," answered the believer.

Just as they were settling down to sleep, there was a horrifying roar from the trees nearby. A lion approached, hungry and on the prowl. The two men were so petrified they could not move. Suddenly the lion attacked, pouncing on the donkey, killing it, and dragging it into the trees to eat it.

The two men eventually climbed a tree to avoid further danger. As they clung to the branches, shaking in their shoes, the skeptic asked, "So, you still think God is good, huh?"

"Of course," said the believer. "Why, if it hadn't been for the donkey, the lion would most surely have attacked us instead. Thanks to the donkey, our lives have been spared."

After a few minutes, when the lion disappeared, the men began to inch down the tree. A shrill cry from the rooster sent them scurrying back up the branches, however. When they looked into their camp, they noticed that a panther had attacked the rooster, caught it, and was devouring it.

"You still think God is good?" asked the skeptic.

"Naturally," came the response of the believer. "Why, if that rooster hadn't let out its cry, you and I might have come down this tree into the waiting jaws of the panther."

Some minutes later, after the danger had passed, the two men were about to sidle down the tree when a strong gust of wind whipped through the camp, destroyed the lantern, and thereby extinguished the flame. They were left in total darkness, unable to move another inch from the tree until morning light.

"And what about this?" asked the skeptic. "Is your God still good?"

For once, the believer was silent.

The next morning, however, the two men descended from the tree and went back to the village for food and provisions. But they found nothing. It seems that a band of robbers had swept into the town the night before, robbed every person in the village, and then fled into the countryside.

"At last," the believer said, "God's ways have been made clear. If we had stayed the night in the inn, we too would have been robbed. If the wind had not destroyed the lantern, the robbers would have seen our light alongside the road and would have robbed us as well. Now are you going to tell me that God isn't good?"

• • •

Logic often eludes a person of faith, but never persistence. Faith may, in fact, be composed more of perspiration than inspiration. This humorous tale reminds us that it is often impossible to reconcile conflicting views of the world. What is required is consistency.

Perhaps this parable might encourage you through the simple realization that if things are bad now—they could always be worse.

The Prince and the Monster
(Buddhist)

Once there was a prince who was very skillful in the ways of war. He knew how to use all his weapons, and he practiced the martial arts diligently.

One day the prince was returning home when he met a monster that had impenetrable skin. The prince shot an arrow at the monster, but it broke against the hide and fell to the ground. The prince threw his spear, but that was ineffective as well. Next he used a javelin, and then a bar. Finally the prince drew his sword and attacked the monster, but the sword broke in half. When all else failed, the prince attacked with his hands and feet, but the monster just picked him up and held him firm in its powerful grip.

"It is no use," the monster said. "Your efforts are ineffective against me. There is nothing you can do. I am going to devour you."

But the prince answered with confidence, "You only think you can devour me. But actually, once you eat me, I will destroy you from inside."

Now the prince's courage disturbed the monster to the point where the monster let the prince go. Later the monster came to the prince and requested that he be instructed in this manner of internal war.

•   •   •

The original purpose of the story was to help Buddhist disciples understand that truth will overcome fear. But there is further encouragement to be found in this story on several levels.

First, it is good to remember that initially, fear magnifies our circumstances and makes a problem seem insurmountable. No problem, however, is so immense that it cannot be tamed to some degree. Even a massive problem can be pared down to size a bit at a time.

Additionally, hard work and perspiration do not always solve a problem. Effort alone is not a cure-all. Sometimes we need to look for alternative approaches to a problem or seek to find a more cerebral solution.

Finally, the parable demonstrates that we should never give up on a problem, even if it seems utterly insurmountable or it appears as though every alternative has been explored. With a bit of ingenuity and courage, often a solution can be found.

Three Magic Gifts
(African)

An old man had three sons. When they became men he called them together and sent them into the world.

The three brothers set out but soon wanted to go their separate ways. They agreed, however, to reunite after a year.

At the end of the year, they came together again and the oldest son asked his brothers what they had earned through all of their labors. "I have nothing but a mirror," the youngest replied. "However, it is a magic mirror. When I look into it I can see anywhere in the world instantaneously."

The middle son said, "I have only a pair of sandals. However, these are powerful sandals. Whoever puts them on can walk in an instant to anywhere in the world."

Then the oldest said, "I have obtained only a small pouch of medicine. However, this medicine is so potent it can cure anything."

The oldest then asked the youngest brother to look into his mirror and see how their father was doing. When he gazed into the mirror, he discovered that his father was already dead and buried.

"Quick," said the middle son, "place your feet into my sandals." All three brothers placed their feet on the sandals and at once they were transported to their father's grave.

The oldest son took out his bag and poured the medicine upon the grave. Their father immediately arose from the dead.

Now which of the three sons did the best?

• • •

As is the case with most African parables, this story contains both a lively dose of humor and some penetrating questions. The first of these is: What might love compel us to do? And a second one: How does one measure success?

Of course, given the magical nature of the tale, one has to look within to find the answers. We can be encouraged in the fact that every person is gifted in different ways. There is a uniqueness to life that transcends our similarities. At a basic level, we need each other to complete any task, any journey, or to obtain any goal.

Those who learn how to share what they have acquired (knowledge, wealth, or healing) will find innumerable rewards.

Fear in the Light of Day
(Jewish)

Two fellows were walking along at night and came upon an insect that appeared to glow in the dark. The first fellow was so terrified that he ran and hid behind a rock.

The other fellow reached down, picked up a firefly, and said, "Is this what terrifies you? At night it looks like it is on fire, but when morning comes, you will see that it is nothing but a bug."

It is often the case that we fear most what we cannot see or understand. But when the blinders of fear are removed, or when we see a problem for what it really is, terror disappears. Once we realize that fear only gets in the way of facing a problem, we are free to solve it.

The parable is also indicative of a common experience: we run away from many problems, or try to deal with them only under duress, instead of examining them logically and putting them in their place. Most problems are rarely worth worrying about. Certainly they are not worth losing sleep over. And when we determine that we will deal with a problem in its time and place, it is like having the blinders removed.

Butterflies Are Free
(Native American)

When the Great Spirit watched his creation, he became sad at the thought that someday all the children would grow old and die. He knew they would be like the flowers of the field and would bloom for only a while before losing their beauty and wilting.

Still, it was autumn, and all the colors of the trees and the fields gave the Great Spirit an idea. "I will create something beautiful for the children," he said.

And so the Great Spirit gathered the colors together. He took gold from the sunlight, blue from the sky, white from the cornmeal, gray from the shadows of the running children, green from the leaves of summer, yellow from the leaves of autumn, black from a girl's long hair, and red, purple, and orange he found in the petals of the flowers in the field. The Great Spirit mixed these together in his bag, along with a few songs that he had gleaned from the birds.

The Great Spirit then walked to a meadow, placed his bag on the ground and said, "Come, children. Come and open the bag. I have a present for you."

The children ran to the bag, opened it, and thousands of bright, beautiful butterflies fluttered into the sky. The children were so happy, seeing such beauty.

Suddenly the butterflies began to sing, and the children sang with them. All the songs of laughter filled the air and the world was a happy place.

Just then a songbird flew by and lighted on the Great Spirit's shoulder. The bird whispered in the Great Spirit's ear: "It isn't right that you have taken our songs and given them to these new creatures. After all, they are lovelier than we are. Isn't it only right that the songs belong to us?"

The Great Spirit thought about this and then agreed with the songbird. "It is only right that the songs belong to you," he said. And so the Great Spirit took the songs back and gave them to the birds. That is why they sing.

But of the butterflies the Great Spirit said, "Look at these. For they are beautiful just as they are."

•   •   •

Some stories are beautiful in their own right, and this marvelous parable is one of them. We can find great encouragement by contemplating the beauty and wonder of the world around us.

When we look closely at life, it is amazing how many questions come to mind. How does the butterfly get its color? What makes a bird sing? Do these creatures feel anything for all the joy they bring? How did color and song first enter into the world? Why is there so much happiness and sadness in the world? These are some of the questions found in the parable.

We can go through life asking far less introspective questions than these. But, most of all, we need to be reminded that some things are simply beautiful in their own right.

12

The Lighter Side of Life

Little by little the time goes by,
Short if you sing it, long if you sigh.

—Anonymous

For the most part we approach life as serious business.
After all, there are challenges and stresses, tears and difficulties that we must face.

In spite of these realities, however, it is amazing to note how
much humor we can find in the world's sacred literature, and
among the teachings of various sages, masters, and leaders. Life
may not be a laughing matter, but many have discovered that
laughing does matter. We all need some light moments here and
there.

A sense of humor can help us through a rough spot, or enable
us to find inner peace. A humorous outlook can even help us to
deal with life's absurdities and injustices.

Take, for example, the student who came to the rabbi to
inquire about pursuing rabbinical studies. "What are your qual-
ifications?" asked the teacher.

The student responded, "I have a high degree of discipline. I
can sleep on the ground, and I can eat grass if I have to. I have
also subdued my body by relinquishing it to the whip no less
than three times a day."

"In that case," said the teacher, "you are far more qualified
to be an ass than a rabbi."

Judaism and Islam, in particular, exhibit a heightened sense of humor, and have perfected the art of poking fun at the idiosyncrasies of Jewish and Islamic faith and culture. No matter what our walk of life, it is important to be able to laugh at ourselves and not take ourselves too seriously.

The parables in this closing chapter will most certainly elicit a chuckle or two—and may even provoke some strong thoughts. After all, laughter can be used to teach and to heal. The parables in this section do this remarkably well.

Breathe deeply. Take these stories in.

Exit laughing.

The Secret of the White Trousers
(Hassidic)

There was a young disciple of Rabbi Naftali who observed that his master always wore white trousers. He asked the rabbi about this.

"I cannot tell you why I wear white trousers," the rabbi answered. "It is a divine secret."

This answer, however, fueled the fire of the young man's curiosity. He pestered the rabbi night and day.

Exhausted by the pupil's questions, the rabbi finally conceded, "All right. I'll tell you the secret . . . after you fast for six days."

The young man willingly agreed, and at the end of the six days he returned to the rabbi.

The rabbi said, "First you must swear that you will not tell another soul this secret as long as you live."

The pupil swore an oath, and then watched as the rabbi went from room to room, locking every door and bolting every window. At last the rabbi came near, leaned toward the young man and whispered, "The reason I wear white trousers is because they are the cheapest!"

"What?!" screamed the pupil. "This is why you had me fast for six days? This is why you locked all the doors and bolted the windows? Why the secrecy?"

"Simple," said the rabbi. "If others discovered this secret, they would all want white trousers. The price would go up. Then where would I be?"

•   •   •

This humorous story reminds us that there is a corner of every religion that should be reserved for laughter. A person can't be serious about prayers, fasting, and observances all the time. After all, God might even be laughing at our efforts. One look in the mirror would tell us that God has a sense of humor.

❧

The Life-Saving Fish
(Sufi)

When Mulla Nasrudin was traveling in India, he came across a yogi living in a hut.

Mulla entered the hut and inquired about the yogi's devotion. The yogi replied, "I have devoted my life to living in communion with all living things—birds, fish, and animals."

"And I as well," Mulla chimed in. "In fact, a fish once saved my life."

"How marvelous," said the yogi. "In all my years of being with my animal friends, I have never heard of such a thing. You must tell me about this."

"Most certainly," Mulla answered. "But I feel I should first learn of your philosophy, so I might explain it better to you."

"Very well," answered the yogi. For days he taught Mulla how to meditate, how to pray, and how to sit in complex postures. Then he asked again about this fish that had saved Mulla's life.

"Well," replied Mulla. "I'm not sure I should tell you about this fish, now that I understand your philosophy."

"But please!" begged the yogi. "To learn about such a fish—a creature that could converse with a man and save his life. Surely such a fish would be one of the highest of God's creatures."

"Perhaps," Mulla responded. "But I'm not sure our philosophies will match. You see, the fish really did save my life. I was about to die of starvation. I caught it, ate it, and lived."

•   •   •

Who's to say how an event might be interpreted or understood? Sometimes the best we can do is tell the story and let others decipher the meaning. Different understandings of the world keep life interesting.

The Case of the Revolving Lawsuit
(Sufi)

A thief was attempting to climb through a window and enter a house in the middle of the night. But when the window frame broke, he fell to the ground below, breaking his legs.

He took the homeowner to court. But the owner said, "Don't sue me, sue the carpenter who made the window."

The carpenter was brought into the court. But the carpenter said, "I'm not to blame. Sue the builder who designed the frame."

The builder was subpoenaed. "Don't sue me," the builder said, "when I was building the frame, a beautiful woman walked by and distracted me. Sue her!"

So the judge subpoenaed the woman. "Is it my fault that I am beautiful?" she said. "If anyone is to blame, it is the one who dyed my dress. It is very bright and colorful and always draws attention."

The judge asked to see the dyer of the dress, saying, "At last, we're going to get to the bottom of this case and see who is truly responsible for this accident."

When the dyer entered the courtroom, however, he turned out to be the woman's husband—and also the thief!

•   •   •

All we have to do is visit a courtroom to see the realism and the twisted humor of this parable. In fact, this story may be so real to some that it's not funny at all!

There are some truths here, however. People are buck passers. Few will take responsibility for their actions—not even thieves caught red-handed in the act. And if there is a loophole to be found, it can probably be discovered in a court of law!

As many have observed through the centuries, there is a stark difference between law and justice. Justice is what we seek. Law is what we get.

In the end, however, we like to believe in the idea that all clandestine acts are eventually discovered, suspects are apprehended, and justice is served. If only the outcomes were as predictable!

The Baal Shem Tov Laughs
(Hassidic)

It was a Friday evening, the beginning of the Sabbath, and the Baal Shem Tov had just given the blessing for the wine when his disciples heard him laugh. Seeing no one else in the room, the disciples wondered what the master had found so funny.

Unwilling to question the Baal Shem Tov at table, the disciples found the master's joy unsettling. After all, the master rarely surrendered to such spontaneity.

The next day, however, one of the disciples asked him why he had laughed the previous day.

"Very well," said the Baal Shem Tov. At that point, he beckoned his disciples to follow him into the country where they traveled to a remote village. The Baal Shem Tov soon asked to see a local bookbinder named Shabti.

The community leader was taken aback by this request, hoping that the master might prefer to see someone more distinguished. "But master," the leader said, "this man is merely a bookbinder. What possible reason would you have for wanting to see him?"

"You shall see," said the Baal Shem Tov.

When the couple arrived—a gray-haired old man and his tottering wife—the Baal Shem Tov greeted them warmly and said, "Now, my friends, tell me what you did last Friday evening at the beginning of the Sabbath. Hide nothing from me, and do not be ashamed."

"Sir," the bookbinder answered, "I will hide nothing from you. And if I have sinned, I pray your forgiveness as from God Himself. All of my life I have worked hard, and through the years I have even been able to put aside a bit of money for my wife and I to celebrate the Sabbath. From the beginning of our marriage it was our custom for my wife to buy all the necessities for the Sabbath—flour, meat, fish, and candles—which she would prepare. Likewise, I have always gone to the house of prayer at the appointed hour and returned to celebrate the Sabbath with my wife.

"Now, as it has happened in these my later years, I have fallen upon meager times. My energy and work have slowed, and I have found it increasingly difficult to provide for the Sabbath celebration out of my means. We had resolved to go without a Sabbath last Friday.

"But as God has blessed us, it turns out that my wife was cleaning the house, sorting through some old clothing, when she discovered some gold and silver buttons. These she took to the goldsmith, who gave her enough money to buy the Sabbath candles and the food. Can you imagine how surprised I was to find a meal waiting for me when I came home? I was so overwhelmed with joy that I bowed to the ground and thanked the Lord for such generosity. Delirious with happiness, I grabbed my wife and we danced around the house, laughing as we went.

"So you see, Master, I have been a silly man, dancing with my wife, acting the part of the fool, and laughing aloud at the mercies of God. If you are ready to dispense a penance, I will accept it in all humility."

When the old bookbinder had finished speaking, the Baal Shem Tov turned to his disciples and said, "Please understand that all the host of heaven rejoiced with this man. I saw all of this and laughed with him."

•   •   •

This parable is one of many traditional tales centered around the life of Rabbi Israel ben Eliezer, a rabbi who lived in Europe during the mid-1700s, and is commonly regarded as the founder of the Hassidic tradition of Judaism. This rabbi became known as the Baal Shem Tov, which means "the master of (God's) name."

As with many parables relating to the Sabbath, this story contains an element of mystery and happiness. Though not all people observe a day of rest, this legend points to the surprising joy that can be found in keeping faith with one's traditions and the simple pleasures of celebrating family and home. As the parable reveals, celebrating and dancing is much closer to what God desires of us than is heavy-hearted observance of propriety and detail. Laughter brings us closer to God than weeping. Joy is the atmosphere of heaven. There is always a need for the child-like in life, and without laughter we are not living in the fullness of our humanity.

The Value of an Insult
(Desert Fathers)

There was a disciple who studied under a noted Greek philosopher. The philosopher commanded the disciple to give money to everyone who insulted him. When his period of instruction was over, the master told the pupil, "Go to Athens and you will learn what true wisdom is."

The disciple departed, and when he arrived at Athens he found a wise man sitting at the city gate, insulting all who entered the city. This wise man also insulted the disciple as he passed by. But the disciple laughed.

"What's so funny about being insulted?" the wise man wanted to know.

"Because," the disciple responded, "for years I have been paying for this kind of treatment, and now you provide it for free."

"Enter the city," said the wise man, "it is all yours."

•   •   •

In the fourth century, the group of eccentric monks known as the Desert Fathers lived an introspective life, one fraught with hardship and sacrifice. Many of their parables reflect this way of life, but also provide a measure of humor unrivaled in any other Christian tradition.

This story has an insightful humor that offers an alternative perspective to suffering. Difficulties are a part of life. Hardship will come. But the one who is able to laugh in the face of these setbacks will emerge not only victorious, but wiser. Sometimes, the best way to face a problem is to laugh at it.

The deepest truth here, however, can be found in the observation that we can prepare ourselves to receive criticism. Just as an athlete might train for months or years for an event— enduring hardship, pain, and criticism—we, too, can become desensitized to the criticism and harsh treatment of others. A bit at a time, we can learn to rise above the hardships we face and learn that we don't have to take all criticism personally.

The Late, Great Rabbi Debate
(Jewish)

One day Rabbi Eliezer was debating his position with ten sages. He used all of his powers of argument and reason, but the other rabbis remained unconvinced. "The majority rules," they said. "It is ten to one."

When Rabbi Eliezer saw that the other sages were not persuaded by logic, he resorted to other tactics. "If I am right," Rabbi Eliezer said, "let this carob tree be uprooted and moved a hundred cubits away." Immediately the carob tree was uprooted and moved a hundred cubits.

The other rabbis were unmoved in their position. "One cannot find proof in a carob tree," they said.

So Rabbi Eliezer said, "If I am right, then let the river prove it by flowing in the opposite direction." Immediately the river began to flow upstream.

The other rabbis shrugged and said, "One cannot find proof in a river, either."

So Rabbi Eliezer said to the other ten sages, "If I am right, then let proof come directly from heaven!" Immediately a voice thundered forth and said to the sages: "Rabbi Eliezer is right. Listen to him!"

One of the sages rose to his feet and said, "All right, Eliezer. Ten to *two!*"

•   •   •

In the biblical book of Genesis, there is a portrait of Abraham arguing with God over the fate of Sodom and Gomorrah. This tradition may provide some of the fodder for the sizable collection of Jewish tales where God shows up to settle a dispute. An important ingredient to God's justice, in Jewish tradition, was the Almighty's willingness to enter into dialogue with human beings. The outcomes in life are not predetermined. There is always room for change.

This parable is a marvelous example of rabbinic debate and the types of discussions typically attributed to rabbinic discourse.

Wanted: Dead or Alive
(Taoist)

Chuang-tzu was fishing in the river when the prince of Ch'u assigned two officials to find him. They were sent to request that Chuang-tzu take charge of the Ch'u state. When the officials arrived, Chuang-tzu continued fishing and offered this remark without looking at them: "I have heard that in Ch'u there is a sacred tortoise that has been dead for three thousand years. I hear that the prince keeps the remains of this creature enclosed in a chest of the ancestral people. What do you think—would this tortoise rather be dead and have its remains worshipped, or be alive and wag its tail in the mud?"

"No doubt, it would rather be alive," the officials responded.

"Yes. And I too will wag my tail in the mud," replied Chuang-tzu.

•   •   •

Two hundred years after the writing of the *Tao te Ching*, a sage by the name of Chuang-tzu lived and taught. His writings became the second most important source for the philosophy of Taoism.

This quaint parable contains some marvelous insights.

First, not all matters are urgent. An emergency on the part of one does not constitute an emergency for another. Some matters are best dealt with in a calm, logical manner.

Second, priorities count. A day spent in relaxation and contemplation may be far more important than taking stock tips or running an empire. Keeping our priorities straight is crucial to our health and well-being. Furthermore, others respect the person who stays true to these commitments.

Finally, integrity keeps everyone honest. It is better to tell the truth and live with the consequences than it is to live with a lie and hate ourselves for the compromise. Better yet, finding a humorous way to approach a serious issue can often disarm would-be attackers. A kind word or a smile often improves a tense situation.

The Rabbi's Clothes
(Jewish)

A rabbi and his pupil were spending the night at a hotel. Before turning in for the night, the student asked the maid to wake him at dawn, since he had an early appointment.

At dawn, the student was awakened by a knock at the door. He rose, thanked the maid, and, not wanting to disturb the rabbi's slumber, began to dress in the dark. In his haste, however, the pupil accidentally put on the rabbi's garments instead of his own, including the rabbi's long coat and distinctive hat.

The student closed the hotel door and hurried to his appointment. On his way, however, he happened to pass by a mirror. Seeing the image in the glass, the student let out a yelp.

"That stupid maid!" he exclaimed, "she woke the rabbi instead of me!"

•   •   •

Sometimes, in our haste, we end up making a situation worse. It is always better to proceed with care and complete a task properly the first time.

We might also benefit, now and then, from a quick glance in the mirror. Learning how to be introspective and self-critical can help us in the long run. It may save us some heartache later on.

The Milk Cow
(Jewish)

A woman once sent her husband to the market to buy a milk cow. When he returned with the animal, the wife went immediately to the barn, milk pail in hand, eager to make butter and cheese. She returned a few minutes later, however, with an empty pail.

Furious with her husband for buying a useless cow, the wife said, "That cow you bought doesn't want to give one drop of milk!"

"Get back," the husband said. "You don't know what you're doing. Let me try." He went to the barn, but returned a few minutes later with an empty pail.

"Well, what did I tell you?" the wife said.

"You should be ashamed of yourself," the husband said. "How can you say that cow doesn't want to give milk? Of course she wants to give milk. But, poor thing, she can't!"

•   •   •

Many Jewish parables, in particular, revel in wordplay. Here the humor revolves around the nuances of language and a simple domestic dispute. There's nothing profound about the tale, but it does have the ring of familiarity to it.

Sometimes—especially in the home—we have to settle for a good effort when we'd rather have results.

Life, Liberty, and the Pursuit of Luggage
(Jewish)

A rabbi was traveling abroad and happened to notice a man who was downcast. "What's wrong?" the rabbi asked.

"I have no interest in life anymore," the man confessed. "I have all the money in the world, and can travel anywhere I want. But there is no place that holds any excitement for me anymore. There is nothing in life that I find compelling or worth pursuing."

When the rabbi heard this, he reached down, grabbed the man's suitcase, and took off running.

Naturally, the man gave pursuit, but the rabbi was fast, and he soon outdistanced the fellow and stopped to wait for him.

When the poor fellow trudged up, out of breath and sweating, he appeared more miserable than before. But as soon as he saw his bag, he ran to it, saw that his belongings were safe, and became extremely happy.

•　　•　　•

The parable reminds us that happiness is a state of mind. Some are unhappy in their excesses. Others are happy in their poverty. Some are bored by a life overflowing with things. Others find excitement and anticipation in the advent of each new day.

Perhaps there is a simple lesson we can learn from this tale: If life has grown weary and dull, shake things up a little. Step out of the tired and the routine. Look for new pursuits—even simple ones that may have been discarded or overlooked. Somewhere in the mix there may be a new adventure.

Many times we don't realize how routine our lives have become and how much we take for granted until we find ourselves in a new situation.

Stinking of Zen
(Zen Buddhist)

A young disciple came to his master's deathbed and asked, "Is there anything else I need to know?"

The dying master replied, "No. And yet there is one thing that worries me."

"And what is that?" asked the disciple.

"The trouble is," said the master, "you stink of Zen."

• • •

This story, attributed to Zen master Hakuin (1686–1769), demonstrates the playful criticism and introspective amusement of Zen teaching. Although other religions might not be so self-critical, we probably know people who stink of Christianity, of Judaism, or Islam. The parable, of course, is addressing narrow-mindedness and pride.

Often, to experience the true essence of a belief, we have to step outside the box. A change of venue may be in order, or a change of heart. Perhaps what is needed is more playfulness, more delight, maybe a bit of awe or humility.

And, as the parable suggests, a dose of humor wouldn't hurt either.

Foul Advice
(Sufi)

A man caught a bird in a trap. But as he reached into the trap to take it out, the bird said, "Sir, you obviously have cows and sheep you could eat instead of me. The little bit of meat on my bones will not satisfy you. I have something far more valuable than my flesh, so if you'll let me go, I'll give you three bits of wisdom. The first I will give while standing on your hand. The second I will offer from your roof. And the third I'll dispense from the limb of that tree."

Since the fellow was interested in the bird's advice, he set it free.

The bird stood on the man's hand and said, "Never believe an absurd remark."

The bird immediately flew away and landed on the rooftop. "My second bit of wisdom is—do not grieve over the past. It is gone! Have no regrets."

Continuing his speech, the bird said, "Incidentally, there is a huge pearl of several pounds inside my body. Had you not set me free, you would have been set for life. You could have owned the largest pearl in the world, but because you set me free, you lost it."

The fellow began to weep and wail over the loss. But the bird spoke up, "Didn't I just tell you—*don't grieve over the past*. And I also said—*never believe an absurd remark*. How could there be a pearl inside my little body weighing several pounds? Does this make sense to you?"

When the fellow regained his composure, he asked the bird, "You promised three bits of advice. Tell me the third."

"Certainly," said the bird. "After all, you've made such good use of the first two."

•   •   •

Another of Rumi's parables, this bit of wisdom offers some sound advice. First, absurdities abound, yet people believe them. Second, the greatest sorrows are those that are centered in the past—moments or incidents that cannot be changed, but which we refuse to release.

What is the third bit of advice? You can figure it out on your own.

Or any bird could tell you.

The Starving Donkey
(Jewish)

There was a stingy fellow who was always trying to save a penny. One day he decided that his donkey was eating too much, so he cut back on the animal's rations a bit each day.

When a neighbor noticed this, the fellow explained, "If I wean the donkey away from his feed a bit at a time, he will adjust."

So, each day, the fellow cut back on the animal's feed. Everything seemed to be going well until the donkey died one day of starvation.

"Too bad," the fellow told his neighbor. "If the donkey hadn't died, I think I could have trained him to eat nothing at all!"

●　　●　　●

Reminiscent of the old adage—an ounce of prevention is worth a pound of cure—this funny tale turns the maxim on its head. Too much of anything is a bad idea. And when it comes to cutting corners, some corners cannot be cut.

The story reminds us that it's best to leave some things as they are. Too much change often produces disastrous results.

The Trouble with Books
(Sufi)

Ibn Yusuf once said: "There are too many people coming to me with their books. Some want my opinion, others ask for my interpretation, and still others have their favorite volumes that they insist I must read. I am at my wit's end."

So Ibn Yusuf went to see a doctor. "Give me something to remedy this problem," he asked.

The doctor gave Yusuf a book. "Show this to people when they bring you other books to read," he said.

Inside the cover was a single sentence: "The time you have wasted reading this sentence could have been better used in some other endeavor."

•   •   •

The words of Ecclesiastes may ring true here: "Of making many books there is no end, and much study makes a person weary." Life is best experienced by interaction. While study has its place, we can also find joy by sharing moments with others, working with our hands, or pursuing favorite pleasures.

Whoppers
(African)

Three storytellers met one day and began to tell stories. Each of them thought he could outdo the others by telling the biggest tale.

The first storyteller said, "I was out in a field and saw two birds fighting. The first bird swallowed the second bird, and the second bird swallowed the first, so that they ended up eating each other."

The next storyteller said, "This is nothing. The other day I was out in the field, and I saw a man who had cut off his own head and had it in his mouth eating it."

The third storyteller said, "I was going to town when I saw a woman coming down the road carrying her house, her farm, and all her worldly possessions on her head. I asked her why she was leaving town. She told me she had heard a horrible story about a man who had cut off his head and had it in his mouth eating it. She was so afraid, she left town."

Now who told the biggest story?

•   •   •

There are parables, and then there are whoppers. The most outlandish tales have the unique power to stimulate our minds. Fantasy and imagination are important. In most walks of life, we are limited only by our vision and creativity—or our lack of it.

What a Fool Believes
(Jewish)

One day a fool came to the rabbi and said, "Rabbi, I know I'm a fool, but I don't know what to do about it."

The rabbi answered, "But if you know you are a fool, then surely you're no fool."

"Then why do people say I am a fool?" the man asked.

After a moment the rabbi answered, "In this case, if your self-assessment is based only on what other people think of you, then surely you are a fool!"

•　　•　　•

This is a wise story for anyone who is easily hurt by other people's comments. But self-esteem can never be based on what other people think. Our motivation and goals should always be directed by the heart, rather than responding to external voices and demands.

Furthermore, those who know themselves cannot be swayed by the hurtful comments of others.

The Tale of a Loincloth
(Traditional Hindu)

A poor ascetic went down to the river to wash his loincloth—which was the only possession he owned. When he hung the loincloth out to dry, he discovered that birds had pecked holes in it. So he went into the village to beg for a new one.

While he was there, however, begging on the streets, someone told him, "You don't need a new loincloth. What you need is a cat to protect the loincloth from the birds."

So the ascetic begged for a cat until he received one.

Naturally, however, after some time, he had to feed the animal. Soon he was begging for milk to feed the cat. "If it's milk you need," one of the villagers told him, "then you should beg for a cow."

The ascetic begged for a cow until someone gave him the animal. This too proved disastrous, for soon the ascetic had to feed the cow. He began to beg for hay. "You need a farm," someone told him.

The ascetic begged until he received a farm. But then he had to have workers to till the soil and plant the seed. Before long, the poor ascetic was doing a brisk business running the place. He married, had children, and spent all of his time thinking about the business.

Much later, the guru came to visit the ascetic, but could find him nowhere. When he inquired in town, someone directed him to the farm. The guru walked into the country, found a big beautiful house, and knocked on the door. When the ascetic answered, the guru asked, "What happened?"

The ascetic fell at his master's feet, begged for mercy, and replied, "It all started with a simple loincloth!"

•   •   •

Sometimes in life, our goals and intentions go awry. We begin a journey with the idea of completing it—but sometimes get lost along the way. We take vows—but break them later on. Or we make plans—but end up getting detoured.

Perhaps this little parable reminds us that focus is a key element in life. There are many distractions, voices, and enticements that can lure us away from what is most important.

As with a diet, one slip with a doughnut or a cookie can often lead to more. Likewise, in life, there are many paths we can take, but if we have chosen a certain road or lifestyle, it is difficult to stay the course—especially if we are trying to live simply, without buying into the consumerist mentality.

The best way to achieve a goal is to stay focused on the basics. Too many distractions can often lead to failure.

Looking for Love
(Sufi)

Mulla Nasrudin was talking with a friend about his love life. "I thought I had found the perfect woman," Mulla said. "She was beautiful and had the most pleasing features a man could imagine. She was exceptional in every way, except she had no knowledge.

"So I traveled farther and met a woman who was both beautiful and intelligent. But, alas, we couldn't communicate.

"After further travels, I met a lady who had everything: perfect mind, perfect intelligence, and a great beauty, all the features I was looking for, but . . . "

"What happened?" asked the friend. "Why didn't you marry her at once?"

"Ah, well," said Mulla, "as luck would have it, she was looking for the perfect man."

•   •   •

Nothing drives a harder bargain than love, especially if we are looking for the perfect person. The way we see another person through the eyes of love also says a great deal about how we see ourselves. If we are looking for a perfect match, we must also be the perfect catch.

The truth is, we don't find custom-fit love in an off-the-rack world.

Willpower
(Buddhist)

A young woman came to the master with a problem. She deeply desired to develop a love for everyone, but she was finding it difficult due to a persistent shopkeeper who continued to harass her. Every day, when the young woman passed through the market, the shopkeeper would pursue her with unwelcome advances. The master asked her to continue to fill her heart with love, even for this man.

One day, however, when the shopkeeper began to harass her, the young woman defended herself by chasing the shop-keeper through the market with her upraised umbrella. As she did this, she noticed the master sitting in the market, watching the spectacle.

The next day the young woman came to the master and asked for forgiveness. "What can I do?" she asked. "How can I fill my heart with love when this one man provokes such anger?"

"What you need to do," said the master, "is fill your heart with love before you go the market. Keep this love in your heart, and when he comes at you, hit him over the head with your umbrella as hard as you can."

•   •   •

Sometimes love must be tough. If we love another person, that doesn't mean we agree to become a doormat. This parable teaches a powerful truth: those who love others fully and deeply have first learned to love and respect themselves. When we demand respect, we actually open the doorway that makes love possible. We should never forget that love makes us stronger people, not weaker people.

Once we have learned to love ourselves, we are free to love others.

Who do you need to love? What candles do you need to light?

Notes on the Parables

The parables in this volume are paraphrases and adaptations of classic stories and traditions. Many of these are traditional tales I have heard, and have retold here. I also used numerous sources to collect other parables, and to that end I include here a source listing of each one. For more information on published sources, see the bibliography.

Introduction

"The Meaning of a Parable." Adapted from the Talmud.
"The Baal Shem Tov's Prayer." Adapted from Buber, *Tales of the Hasidim*.
Title Parable. Traditional story.

1. Family Matters

"The Road to Heaven." Source unknown.
"Enough Fish." Traditional Yiddish tale.
"The Reunion." *The Teaching of Buddha*.
"A Common Good." Based on a Jewish Midrash.
"The Ways of Home." *The Teaching of Buddha*.
"Reconciliation." *The Teaching of Buddha*.
"On Children." Cleary, *The Essential Confucius*.
"One Heart, One Mind." *The Teaching of Buddha*.
"Great Aspirations." Cleary, *The Essential Confucius*.
"The Backyard Marriage." Traditional Jewish tale.
"Marital Riches." Midrash.
"The Lost and the Found." Routledge, *With a Prehistoric People: The Akikuyu of British East Africa*.
"The Greatest of All Illusions." Adapted from Das, *The Snow Lion's Turquoise Mane: Wisdom Tales from Tibet*.
"The Internal Compass." *The Teaching of Buddha*.
"The Wise and the Old." *The Teaching of Buddha*.
"The Blessing of Grandchildren." Adapted from Gaster, *The Exempla of the Rabbis*.

2. Faith to Live By

"The Value of Life." Source unknown.

"The Voice." Traditional Hindu tale.

"A Good Harvest." Adapted from Matt. 13:3–8 Authorized (King James) Version.

"The Fallen Traveler." Source unknown.

"The Quietness of Faith." Traditional Hassidic tale.

"The Best Questions." Adapted from Theophane the Monk, *Tales of a Magic Monastery.*

"A Piece of Truth." Adapted from Hahn, *The Heart of Understanding.*

"The Good Neighbor." Adapted from Luke 10:29–37 Authorized (King James) Version.

"Miraculous Powers." Adapted from Bayet and Jamnia, *Tales from the Land of the Sufis.*

"Small Discoveries." Adapted from Matt. 13:31–32 and Matt. 13:44 Authorized (King James) Version.

"The Religious Fanatic." Source unknown.

"The Meaning of Heaven and Hell." Adapted from Reps, *Zen Flesh, Zen Bones.*

"The Lunatic." Traditional Hindu tale.

"The Banquet of Opportunity." Jewish Midrash.

"Where is the Lord?" Traditional Sufi tale.

"The Value of Religion." Traditional Jewish tale.

"Salvation Has Come." Traditional Hindu tale.

"The Man Who Walked on Water." Source unknown.

"A Jar of Meal." Funk and Hoover, *The Five Gospels.*

3. Hope Springs Eternal

Introductory Parable. *The Teaching of Buddha.*

"A Kind Word." *The Sayings of the Desert Fathers.*

"The Last-Minute Pardon." Oral source.

"A Peace of Mind." Adapted from Hamill and Seaton, *The Essential Chuang Tzu.*

"Hoping for Forgiveness." Waddell, *The Desert Fathers.*

"The Location of Paradise." Traditional Jewish tale.

"The Journey of Togetherness." Adapted from Hewitt, *Parables, Etc.,* vol. 2, no. 11.

"Bound Together." Temple, *Aesop: The Complete Fables.*

"The Rabbi's Daughters." Traditional Yiddish tale.

"Persistence Pays Off." Adapted from Luke 11:5–8 and Luke 18:1–8 Authorized (King James) Version.

"The Singer." Traditional Jewish tale.

"A Circle of Light." Adapted from Shah, *The Subtleties of the Inimitable Nasrudin.*

"The Banker and the Skeptic." Source unknown.

"God's Banquet." Robert J. Miller, *The Complete Gospels*.
"Snail's Pace." Traditional Sufi tale.
"Letting Go." Traditional tale.

4. *The Love That Conquers All*

Introductory parable. Source unknown.
"The Cup and the Comb of Jesus." Traditional Sufi tale.
"The White Elephant and the Hunter." *The Teaching of Buddha*.
"The Men in the Mirror." Adapted from Kierkegaard, *The Parables of Kierkegaard*.
"The Heart of Love." Traditional Jewish tale.
"Inner Nature." *The Teaching of Buddha*.
"The Fire of Compassion." *The Teaching of Buddha*.
"The Jewel of Creation." Talmud.
"Portraits of the World." Kierkegaard, *The Parables of Kierkegaard*.
"The Three Rings." Traditional Jewish tale.
"A Vision of Heaven and Hell." Traditional Jewish tale.
"Muhammad and the Cat." Traditional Islamic tale.

5. *The Power of Friendship*

Introductory parable. Adapted from Nomura, *Desert Wisdom*, rev. ed.
"The Eagle's Eggs." Adapted from Smith and Dale, *The Ila-Speaking Peoples of Northern Rhodesia*.
"Two Friends and a Bear." Temple, *Aesop: The Complete Fables*.
"An Image of Peacefulness." Adapted from Nomura, *Desert Wisdom*.
"Friendship Is Its Own Reward." Adapted from White, *Stories for the Journey*.
"A Day and Night." Adapted from Silverman, *Rabbinic Wisdom and Jewish Values*.
"The Ant and the Pigeon." Temple, *Aesop: The Complete Fables*.
"Friendly Advice." *The Teaching of Buddha*.
"The Burden by the River." Adapted from Schloegl, *The Wisdom of the Zen Masters*.
"A Stone's Throw." Adapted from the Talmud.
"The Greatest Treasure." Silverman, *Rabbinic Wisdom and Jewish Values*.
"The Difference between a Ditch and a Mound." Oral source.
"Many Roots." Talmud.
"Bearing the Burden." *The Teaching of Buddha*.
"The Patience of a Friend." Talmud.

6. *Embracing the Freedom to Live*

"True Enlightenment." Reps, *Zen Flesh, Zen Bones*.
"Matters of the Heart." Traditional Jewish tale.
"The Poor Artist." *The Teaching of Buddha*.

"Opening Doors." Adapted from Hahn, *Zen Keys*.
"The Bracelets of Buddhahood." *The Teaching of Buddha*.
"A Life of Leisure." Adapted from the Talmud.
"The Mystery of the Palm Wine." Traditional African and Near Eastern tale.
"The Lesson of the Nerrah Tree." Oral source.
"The Coconut Trap." Traditional Hindu tale.
"Metamorphosis." Adapted from Giles, *Chuang Tzu: Mystic, Moralist, and Social Reformer*.
"The Magic Purse." Traditional Jewish tale.

7. Finding the Wisdom Within

Introductory parable. Adapted from the Talmud.
"That Is What You Are." The Upanishads.
"The Character of Leadership." Confucius, *The Analects of Confucius*.
"A Solid Foundation." *The Teaching of Buddha*.
"Be Prepared at All Times." Adapted from Matt. 25:1–13 Authorized (King James) Version.
"A Box, a Cane, and a Pair of Shoes." *The Teaching of Buddha*.
"Two Wise Stories from Avianus." My translations from *Loeb Classical Library: Minor Latin Poets*.
"A Leaf from the Tree of Knowledge." Traditional Yiddish tale.
"The Essence of Time." *The Teaching of Buddha*.
"One Wise Meatball." Adapted from Canonge, *Comanche Texts*.
"The Visitation." *The Teaching of Buddha*.
"Going to the Dogs." Adapted from the Talmud.
"A Honey Pot of Wisdom." *The Teaching of Buddha*.
"The Fox and the Vineyard." Adapted from the Talmud.
"The Success of the Three Maestros." Giles, *Chuang Tzu*.
"The Talking Skull." Traditional African tale.
"The Wisdom of Crows." Traditional Japanese tale.
"The Reminder." Temple, *Aesop: The Complete Fables*.
"The World and More." Giles, *Chuang Tzu*.
"Personal Perspective." Source unknown.
"Appearances Can Be Deceiving." Hamill, *The Essential Chuang Tzu*.
"The Snake and the Treasure." Talmud/Midrash.
"A Big Fish in a Small Pond." Mitchell, *Tao Te Ching: A New English Version*.

8. Seeing the Possiblities

"Hurry Up and Wait." Schloegl, *The Wisdom of the Zen Masters*.
"A Better Life." Traditional Yiddish tale.
"In Retrospect." Traditional Jewish tale.
"The Last of the Golden Eggs." Temple, *Aesop: The Complete Fables*.
"A Greater Reward." *The Teaching of Buddha*.
"The Nightingale and the Peacock." Shah, *The Magic Monastery*.

"The Leper and Elijah." Traditional tale.
"The Burden by the Side of the Road." Traditional Sufi tale.
"Come Together." Traditional African tale.
"The Eyes Have It." Adapted from the Talmud.
"The Way of Forgetfulness." Cleary, *The Essential Tao*.
"The Tattooed Sailor." Adapted from Miller and Kenedi, *God's Breath*.
"Three Talented Friends." Oral source.
"The Wisdom of God." Adapted from Knowles, *Folk-Tales of Kashmir*.
"All Things Are Possible." Adapted from Shah, *The Pleasantries of the Incredible Mulla Nasrudin*.

9. Seeking a Guiding Light

"How to Become a Buddha." *The Teaching of Buddha*.
"The Meaning of Work." Merton, *The Wisdom of the Desert*.
"How to Have a Good Argument." Adapted from Levin, *Classic Hassidic Tales*.
"Sand Castles." *The Teaching of Buddha*.
"The Pearl." Funk and Hoover, *The Five Gospels*.
"Heads and Tails." *The Teaching of Buddha*.
"The Courageous Fox." Talmud/Midrash.
"How to Capture the Wind." Merton, *The Wisdom of the Desert*.
"A Bowl by Any Other Name." Traditional Zen tale.
"The Most Valuable Thing in the World." Adapted from the writings of Rumi.
"The Riddle of the Strongest." Adapted from 1 Esdras 3:1–4:42 Authorized (King James) Version.
"What the Caged Bird Knows." Adapted from the Talmud.
"Lord Krishna's Request." Traditional Hindu tale.
"The Meaning of Progress." Cleary, *The Essential Tao*.

10. The Strength of a Virtuous Life

"The Great Way." Griffith, ed., *Confucius: The Analects*.
"Simplicity of Virtue." Adapted from Breuilly and Palmer, *The Book of Chuang Tzu*.
"On Kindness to Animals." Abdullah and Al-Suhrawardy, *The Sayings of Muhammad*.
"A Drink of Water." *The Teaching of Buddha*.
"The Contest." Traditional Chinese tale.
"Service." Bayet and Jamnia, *Tales From the Land of the Sufis*.
"The Beauty of Kindness." Adapted from Novak, *Fairy Tales From Japan*.
"A Time of Power." Breuilly and Palmer, *The Book of Chuang Tzu*.
"The Silver Window." Silverman, *Rabbinic Wisdom and Jewish Values*.
"Feeding Chickens." Traditional Jewish tale.
"The Donkey's Disguise." Indian tale.
"A Refusal of Sweetness." Baha u'llah, *Gleanings From the Writings of Baha u'llah*.

11. *The Gentle Art of Encouragement*

"The Return of the Prodigal Son." Adapted from Luke 15:11–32 Authorized
  (King James) Version.

"Spitting on the Rabbi." Adapted from Frankel, *The Classic Tales: 4000 Years
  of Jewish Lore.*

"God is Good." Traditional Jewish tale.

"The Prince and the Monster." *The Teaching of Buddha.*

"Three Magic Gifts." Adapted from Cardinall, *Tales Told in Togoland.*

"Fear in the Light of Day." Adapted from the Talmud.

"Butterflies Are Free." Traditional Native American myth.

12. *The Lighter Side of Life*

"The Secret of the White Trousers." Adapted from Langer, *Nine Gates.*

"The Life-Saving Fish." Adapted from Shah, *The Exploits of the Incomparable
  Mulla Nasrudin.*

"The Case of the Revolving Lawsuit." Traditional Sufi tale.

"The Baal Shem Tov Laughs." Traditional Hassidic tale.

"The Value of an Insult." Traditional Desert Fathers tale.

"The Late, Great, Rabbi Debate." Talmud/oral tradition.

"Wanted, Dead or Alive." Adapted from Mair, *Wandering the Way: Early Taoist
  Tales and Parables of Chuang Tzu.*

"The Rabbi's Clothes." Traditional Jewish tale.

"The Milk Cow." Adapted from Ausubel, *A Treasury of Jewish Folklore.*

"Life, Liberty, and the Pursuit of Luggage." Traditional Jewish tale.

"Stinking of Zen." Source unknown.

"Foul Advice." Adapted from a traditional tale of Rumi.

"The Starving Donkey." Traditional Jewish tale.

"The Trouble with Books." Adapted from Shah, *The Magic Monastery.*

"Whoppers." Adapted from Abrahams, *African Folktales.*

"What a Fool Believes." Traditional Jewish tale.

"The Tale of a Loincloth." Traditional Hindu tale.

"Looking for Love." Adapted from Shah, *The Subtleties of the Inimitable
  Nasrudin.*

"Willpower." Traditional Buddhist tale.

Bibliography

Among the dozens of books I used to gather information for this collection, the following books were especially helpful. I am grateful to the various translators, authors, and publishers of these works.

Abdullah, Allama Sir and Al-Mamum Al-Suhrawardy. *The Sayings of Muhammad*. New York: Citadel Press, 1990.

Abrahams, Roger. *African Folktales*. New York: Pantheon Books, 1983.

Ausubel, Nathan. *A Treasury of Jewish Folklore*. New York: Crown, 1948.

Baha u'llah. *Gleanings from the Writings of Baha u'llah*. Wilmette, Ill.: The Bahá'í Publishing Trust, 1976.

Bayet, Mojdeh and Mohammad Ali Jamnia. *Tales from the Land of the Sufis*. Boston: Shambhala Publications, 1994.

Breuilly, Elizabeth and Martin Palmer. *The Book of Chuang Tzu*. New York: Penguin Putnam, 1996.

Buber, Martin. *Tales of the Hasidim*. New York: Schocken Books, 1948.

Canonge, Elliott. *Comanche Texts*. Vol. 1. Linguistic Series. Norman, Okla.: Summer Institute of Linguistics of the University of Oklahoma, 1958.

Cardinall, A. W. *Tales Told in Togoland*. London: Oxford University Press, 1931.

Cleary, Thomas. *The Essential Confucius*. New York: HarperCollins, 1992.

——— . *The Essential Tao*. San Francisco: Harper, 1991.

Confucius. *The Analects of Confucius*. Translated by James Legge. 1897.

Das, Surya. *The Snow Lion's Turquoise Mane: Wisdom Tales from Tibet*. New York: HarperCollins, 1992.

Eberhard, Wolfram. *Folktales of China*. Chicago: University of Chicago Press, 1965.

Erdoes, Richard and Alfonso Ortiz. *American Indian Trickster Tales*. New York: Viking Press, 1998.

Fadiman, James and Robert Frager. *Essential Sufism*. Edison, N.J.: Castle Books, 1997.

Frankel, Ellen. *The Classic Tales: 4000 Years of Jewish Lore*. Northvale, N.J.: Jason Aronson, Inc., 1989.

Funk, Robert and Roy Hoover. *The Five Gospels*. New York: Polebridge Press, 1993.

Gaster, Moses. *The Exempla of the Rabbis*. London: Asia Publishing, 1924.

Giles, Herbert A., trans. *Chuang Tzu: Mystic, Moralist, and Social Reformer.* London: Bernard Quaritich, 1989.

Griffith, Tom, ed. *Confucius: The Analects.* Hertfordshire, England: Wordsworth Editions, 1996.

Hahn, Thich Naht. *The Heart of Understanding.* Albany, Calif.: Parallax Press, 1988.

———. *Zen Keys.* New York: Image Books, 1995.

Hamill, Sam and J. P. Seaton. *The Essential Chuang Tzu.* Boston: Shambhala Publications, 1999.

Hewitt, James, *Parables, Etc.,* vol. 2, no. 11, 1984.

Kierkegaard, Søren. *The Parables of Kierkegaard.* Edited by Thomas C. Oden. Princeton, N.J.: Princeton University Press, 1978.

Knowles, J. Hinton. *Folk-Tales of Kashmir,* 2nd ed. London: Kegan Paul, Tranch, Trübner, and Company, 1893.

Kornfield, Jack and Christina Feldman. *Soul Food.* New York: HarperCollins, 1996.

Langer, J. *Nine Gates.* Northvale, N.J.: Jason Aronson, Inc., 1993.

Levin, Meyer. *Classic Hassidic Tales.* New York: Viking Press, 1975.

Mair, Victor H. *Wandering the Way: Early Taoist Tales and Parables of Chuang Tzu.* Honolulu: University of Hawaii Press, 1998.

Merton, Thomas. *The Wisdom of the Desert.* New York: W. W. Norton and Co., 1988.

Miller, John and Aaron Kenedi, eds. *God's Breath.* New York: Marlowe, 2000.

Miller, Robert J. *The Complete Gospels.* Sonoma, Calif.: Polebridge Press, 1994.

Mitchell, Stephen. *Tao Te Ching: A New English Version.* New York: HarperCollins, 1988.

Nomura, Yushi. *Desert Wisdom,* rev. ed. Maryknoll, N.Y.: Orbis Books, 2001.

Novak, Miroslav. *Fairy Tales from Japan.* London: Hamlyn Press, 1976.

Novak, Philip. *The World's Wisdom.* New York: HarperCollins, 1995.

Radin, Paul. *African Folktales.* New York: Schocken Books, 1983.

Reps, Paul. *Zen Flesh, Zen Bones.* New York: Doubleday, 1981.

Routledge, W. S. and Kay. *With a Prehistoric People: The Akikuyu of British East Africa.* London: Frank Cass Publishers, 1910.

The Sayings of the Desert Fathers. Kalamazoo, Mich.: Cistercian Publications, 1972.

Schloegl, Irmgard. *The Wisdom of the Zen Masters.* New York: New Directions, 1975.

Shah, Idries. *The Exploits of the Incomparable Mulla Nasrudin.* London: Octagon Press, 1983.

———. *The Magic Monastery.* London: Octagon Press, 1981.

———. *The Pleasantries of the Incredible Mulla Nasrudin.* New York: Penguin Putnam, 1968.

———. *The Subtleties of the Inimitable Nasrudin.* London: Octagon Press, 1989.

Silverman, William. *Rabbinic Wisdom and Jewish Values*. New York: Union of American Hebrew Congregations Press, 1971.

Smith, Edwin and A. M. Dale. *The Ila-Speaking Peoples of Northern Rhodesia*. New York: Carol Publishing, 1966.

The Teaching of Buddha. Tokyo: Bukkyo Dendo Kyokai, 1966.

Temple, Olivia and Robert. *Aesop: The Complete Fables*. New York: Penguin Books, 1998.

Theophane the Monk. *Tales of a Magic Monastery*. New York: Crossroad/Continuum, 1981.

Waddell, Helen. *The Desert Fathers*. New York: Vintage, 1998.

Warmington, E. H., ed. *Loeb Classical Library: Minor Latin Poets*. Cambridge, Mass.: Harvard University Press, 1995. Author's translations.

White, William R. *Stories for the Journey*. Minneapolis: Augsburg Publishing House, 1988.

Wilson, Epiphanius. *The Wisdom of Confucius*. New York: Crown, 1982.

Zerah, Aaron. *The Soul's Almanac*. New York: Tarcher/Putnam, 1998.

About the Author

Todd Outcalt is a United Methodist pastor who lives and writes in Indianapolis. In addition to his interests in basketball and weight lifting, he is also the author of nine books. His other titles include *The Best Things in Life Are Free* and *Before You Say "I Do."*